MW01282361

Funny That Way

Funny That Way

Adventures in Fabulousness

by Joel Perry

alyson books
los angeles | new york

© 2001 BY JOEL PERRY. ALL RIGHTS RESERVED.

MANUFACTURED IN THE UNITED STATES OF AMERICA.

THIS TRADE PAPERBACK ORIGINAL IS PUBLISHED BY ALYSON PUBLICATIONS,
P.O. BOX 4371, LOS ANGELES, CALIFORNIA 90078-4371.
DISTRIBUTION IN THE UNITED KINGDOM BY
TURNAROUND PUBLISHER SERVICES LTD.,
UNIT 3, OLYMPIA TRADING ESTATE, COBURG ROAD, WOOD GREEN,
LONDON N22 6TZ, ENGLAND.

FIRST EDITION: DECEMBER 2000

01 02 03 04 05 a   10 9 8 7 6 5 4 3 2 1

ISBN 1-55583-557-0

LIBRARY OF CONGRESS CATALOGING-IN-PUBLICATION DATA
    PERRY, JOEL.
      FUNNY THAT WAY : ADVENTURES IN FABULOUSNESS / BY JOEL
    PERRY.—1ST ED.
        ISBN 1-55583-557-0
        1. HOMOSEXUALITY—HUMOR. 2. GAY MEN—HUMOR. 3. GAY WIT AND
    HUMOR. I. TITLE.
    PN6231.H57 P47 2000
    818'.602—DC21   00-046436

COVER PHOTOGRAPHY AND DESIGN BY PHILIP PIROLO.

To God, for giving me all this stuff—
but especially for blessing me with my Fred.

Contents

Acknowledgments

A special thank-you to all those who supported and put up with me while writing this. My wonderful birth family, who are still shaking their heads over this. My editor, Scott Brassart, for holding my hand and for laughing. Monica Trasandes at *Frontiers* magazine for giving me the forum to be silly in newsprint, Gabriel Goldberg and Ben R. Rogers and the guys at *Instinct* magazine for giving me the forum to be silly in glossy print. The Cutler gang for their input: Robert, Rosie, Albert, Pete, Warren, Glenn, Gil and Stephen. My first fans: Mary and Jim, Curtis, Donnie, Katie, Oscar, Wendy, Marshall and Karla, Jack and Michael, and the one who shares my life and soul, my only, my dearest, my Fred.

Preface

OK, my editor said I needed to tell you a few things about me before you plunged into the ensuing pages, although my feeling is, you'd figure out the important stuff. The facts are simple: I'm a gay man living in Los Angeles with two cats and my dear Fred, who has been my spouse since 1980—don't ask me why. I grew up in North Carolina, where I majored in theater. In that state it's the same as wearing a sign that says BIG FAG. Still, I didn't admit to myself I was gay until my early 20s despite a life full of red flags that kept popping up like it was May Day in China. Can you say "wasted time"?

These days I work in syndicated radio with the likes of Dr. Laura and Rush Limbaugh and frequently wake up feeling dirty about it. I try to tell myself, at least we're all doing comedy. To atone, I keep politically active, attend church, point out the picture of Fred on my desk to anyone who comes near, and write silly articles for queer magazines. When no one is looking, I like to eat ham.

My editor also subtitled this book *Adventures in Fabulousness*. Can anyone not named Minnelli live up to that?

PART ONE
Getting to Know Me

HOW I FOUND MY FETISHES

For years I wondered why I was the way I was. Not wondering why I was gay. Please, I knew the reason for that: I needed a challenge I could meet with flair, and I got lucky. But I did wonder why I was the kind of gay I turned out to be. What shaped my turn-ons, rang my chimes, fired my blood and sent it places that upset my Sunday School teachers so?

I spent my formative years in Jacksonville, N.C., home to Camp Lejeune, so most of our baby-sitters were—are you ready for this—U.S. Marines. I remember one in particular. He was named Charlie Brown, and he gave my brother and me horsey rides *in uniform*. Could you die? I was in the fourth grade, so there was nothing going on, but by the time Mama and Daddy got back I was bouncing off the walls for no reason I could possibly have understood. Now I do. I was a military fetishist at the tender age of nine. Sometimes my brother and I would sit on Charlie Brown's lap while we watched *Gomer Pyle, U.S.M.C.* Charlie Brown and my brother would laugh at Gomer, but I'd be squirming and staring at Sergeant Carter on TV like I would later stare at Zak Spears on video. Thus began a lifetime of searching for—and finding—gay fantasies that would sow the seeds of my current kinks.

My mother worked for our neighbor, Miss Ginger, who was a florist. There were numerous deliveries to be made to Camp Lejeune, and I went with my mother after school and on weekends when she drove the delivery van onto the base. It's a wonder I didn't break my neck leaning out the window to stare at all those juicy jarheads. I looked like a dog out for a drive. One time the van broke down and a passing platoon in nothing but sweaty shorts and boots pushed us *five miles* to the nearest base service station. I had my awestruck face pressed against the back window watching dozens of sweaty, shirtless men take turns pushing and then falling back in line as ordered, only to be replaced by new glistening Marines. I felt like Cleopatra on her barge, only better. She had her scraggly slaves, but I was surrounded by tropical flowers in a van with the U.S. Marine Corps on my rear bumper. Push, you maggots, push!

Next door to us lived Larry, the (to me) worldly and mature 16-year-old who every Saturday morning during the spring and summer came outside in only his swim trunks to wash his father's car right next to our side window. I was in fifth grade then, and my Saturday agenda was breakfast, *Huckleberry Hound, The Bugs Bunny Hour,* and "The Larry Gets Soapy and Sweaty and Bends Over a Lot Scrubbing Spectacular." When he was done and he thought nobody was looking, he'd put the hose down his trunks, front and back, again and again. Then he'd go inside and not come back to dry off the car until halfway through *Yogi Bear,* but by then he'd have new shorts and a T-shirt on, so I didn't bother to watch. I liked Yogi Bear. I think I wanted to be Boo-Boo, and I'm too ashamed to tell you where that line of thinking goes.

Books provided plenty of other thrilling possibilities. I wonder if I was the only grade schooler getting off on Curious George. It was more his sense of fun and childlike discovery that captivated me than the animal thing, although I admit I am drawn to the hairier types, especially if they behave like animals in private. And God knows I was at least as curious as George. A couple of years later, at 13, when my mother's hairdresser exposed himself to me, I was not only curious, I knew *exactly* what to do. Shocked the hell out of him. Mother has yet to recover.

Around that time I was finding gay goodies in another entire series of books. Can we talk about the Hardy Boys? While reading *The Secret of You-Fill-In-the-Blank,* I used to dream I was chubby but good-natured Chet, their best friend. I thought it was because I wanted to be their pal and help them solve mysteries. Looking back, I know it was because I wanted to be the meat in a Frank and Joe sandwich. Isn't that cute? Only 13 but ready for a three-way!

In ninth grade we had a macho student gym teacher named Mr. Buchner, who was about 22, stocky but trim, muscular, and very hairy. Our class was the last of his day so he would often shower with us—*shower* being a verb that included horseplay, towel popping, and grab-ass. I would really like to know what the hell was going on. And what was Mr. Buchner thinking when he decided to strip in front of a bunch of ninth-graders, half of whom hadn't even sprouted hair (my half, natch)? Whatever the reason, he was hirsute fantasy fuel until Brush Creek Videos came on the scene.

Then, though, I was happy for any exposure of male flesh. Bare skin was so hard to come by when I was growing up. Now it's as easy as the nearest Calvin Klein ad. (Who would have guessed you needed to be naked to sell clothes?) These days there are plenty of exposed bodies to ogle on CDs too. I had to settle for album covers like the one for the group Steam where a bunch of gangly dorks with dented-in chests were sitting around a steam room (Steam: Get it?) looking for all the world like Monday night at the Melrose Baths...only 40 years younger. Later came the Village People with David the open-shirted construction worker, Victor the open-shirted cop, Randy the open-shirted cowboy...you get the trend. Glenn didn't even wear a shirt; he wore leather and chains, which frightened me terribly, gave me disturbing dreams, and kept me in the bathroom much longer than necessity dictated.

All of this was wonderfully formative. It explains the military thing and my attractions to older men, hairy men, bears (cartoon and otherwise), leather, and disco. In the debate between nature and nurture, my nature was that I was going to be gay, darling, very gay. I have my environment to thank, though, for exactly how it came to be shaped and expressed. So thank you, thank you, thank you, you wacky environment, you! If Mom and Dad had known what they were providing me with, I'm sure they'd have shipped me off to live in an igloo, and what a waste that would have been. Given my gay genes, I'm sure I'd be writing about older Inuits, smooth men, bears (polar and otherwise), and a wardrobe of fabulous fur coats. But I lived where I did and I encountered who and what I did, and that is why, in the words of Harvey Fierstein-cum-Popeye, I yam what I yam.

Now if only I could figure out where that Judy Garland thing comes from.

HOW I THINK (I THINK)

I am forever exasperated with the mind I have. I can tell you the difference between apogee and perigee, but I can't tell you why I'm standing in the middle of the frozen food aisle staring at sugar peas. I know vaguely how the internal combustion engine in my car works, but I don't know how to change the oil or, usually, where it's parked. I can recite "Roof Space," an idiotic patter song from the little-known 1967 Sherlock Holmes Broadway musical *Baker Street,* but I can't recite the three things I came to the grocery to buy. I blame my overly retentive long-term memory cells.

I would love to be able to take these cells that stubbornly retain my ninth-grade locker combination, dump them out like a desk drawer, and fill them with something useful like how to get red wine out of wool or rewire a vibrator.

It's not like I'm asking for anything new. My short-term memory works that way all the time. When I bought my car I checked into all the numbers and ratios and other tedious guy stuff, but once the decision was made, I dumped every well considered reason I bought it as irrelevant information to keep. When people ask me what kind of mileage I get, I have no idea, because now I don't think in those terms. I get ten days a tank. How much horsepower does it have? I don't feel a need to know or care. At any rate, my knowing the figure doesn't change the way the car performs. How many square feet in my apartment? Not many. Three. Enough for two people and two cats. What kind of TV do I have? Square.

Refrigerator? White. The kind that calls my cats when I open it.

Some things I don't even try to learn. When people talk about things like BTUs and RPMs my mind goes AWOL. I have no idea what kind of return I get on my IRA. I know it's not going to be enough, so why carry that information around to be stressed over? What's my HMO? Depends on the day. At my current job it has changed five times, and I have seen no doctor more than once. We're in the process of being bought—again—so I'm sure it will be something else before long. Thanks to our health care system, I am more intimate with pen pals than doctors.

What bothers me is not what I don't know, it's the amazing array of utterly useless information I carry in my head. I know myzopodidae are Old World sucker-footed bats. I am unsure, however, exactly where the Old World is, so don't expect me to point one of these myzopodidae out to you. Sometimes, when I'm bored talking to someone, I turn the conversation to sucker-footed bats. When I do, the person invariably goes away, so I guess it's not totally wasted knowledge. But still...

I somehow managed to learn the group names of many animals but have no occasion to demonstrate this knowledge. Were I to see a leap of leopards I would be too busy running in the opposite direction to display any such learning. A knot of toads sounds like something Elvira cooked up to feed the gals while they all watch *Charmed*. This is the kind of learning that gains one no respect. During a Discovery Channel show on Alaska I pointed out to Fred that bears in a group are called a sloth of bears. An hour later, watching the following show about the rain forest, he said, "Look, Joel, a bear of sloths."

There are other annoying quirks in my brain too. Unlike everyone I know, I don't remember time in a linear fashion. I can tell you what happened, how, and usually where, but forget about my telling you when. I don't remember when I got together with Fred, but it was the year Kubrick's *The Shining* came out. I remember that because it was the last movie I saw with my ex. The breakup was so painful that I ran to the theater to see it three more times because it was the only thing that made me feel better about my situation. Even though I felt like hell, at least I wasn't trapped in a hotel with Shelley Duvall. A month later Fred and I clicked, and it has been nothing but bliss since—and if you believe that, you have never been in a long-term relationship.

In my life, time is like a Lava lamp. Events bubble, merge, float by, and fade, only to recur in another abstract form. Also, I'm unsure whether my life, like a Lava lamp, is fashionable, newly retro, or merely kitsch.

Fred and I went to England twice, but my memory smashes both vacations together so that it seems like one long bout of indigestion and ale. Somehow the pier at Brighton overlaps the weir at Bath and I'm still able to go see a bad London musical that same evening. Another year I went to Paris, but I couldn't tell you when other than to say it was back when I had a 32-inch waist. Surely I ought to be able to dump my knowledge of, say, Alexander the Great to free up those brain cells so I could remember dates from my own life. After all, it's not like I'm going to meet Alexander, and it is constantly embarrassing to have to turn to Fred every time I'm asked, "When did you move to L.A.?"

You might be tempted to ask how I made it through school with such a mind. I made up mnemonics, the equivalent of mental cheat sheets. In chemistry we were to be tested on the periodic chart. I learned it in a fashion that got me a perfect test score and taught me nothing. How? I memorized the columns phonetically. The first group on the left of the chart, going down, I pronounced "hulinakuh-rubsessfrah," which stood for the elements H, Li, Na, K, Rb, Cs, and Fr. The noble gases, on the other side, are He, Ne, Ar, Kr, Xe, and Rn, or "heenee-arker-zeerun." I have retained nothing as to what those abbreviations stand for and have no idea why some gases are noble and others are not. (My guess is it has something to do with scientists working in close quarters and what they had for lunch.) Group 2 on the chart is pronounced "beemug-casir-bara." It might as well be "abracadabra" because, poof!—it provided my only A+ in chemistry. It was a triumph second only to convincing Betty Swails during an experiment that I'd spilled hydrochloric acid on her. She ran screaming to the safety shower at the front of the room, which drenched both her and the teacher's desk. I was punished excessively because the teacher felt I lacked remorse. She was right.

In physics I had to learn the Greek alphabet. I put it to the ABC song, got it correct on the exam, and as a result passed the course. At least the Greek alphabet comes in handy for me; I do crossword puzzles. As for the rest of physics, forget about it. As far as I'm concerned, a light switch is black magic.

This mishmash of a brain defies my attempts to force it to work as I would like. I've tried making lists of things to memorize in order to improve my short-term memory, but I forget what I did with the lists. I've tried learning logical progression by playing chess, but every piece moves a different way and never the way I want it to move—which I've been told I take far too personally. I've given up all hope of balancing my checkbook because every math class I ever took was a waste of pencil lead and sweat. I don't know what the fuss is all about. No one I know even uses math. They use calculators.

I wish someone had been able to x-ray my head in high school and say, "Boy, is this one a mess. Civics and history are a lost cause, and just look at that hypothalamus! Why, P.E. could kill this boy!" I could have spent the time wasted in useless core curricula learning something I could actually use like, oh, I don't know, sewing leather. If only the guidance counselor had been able to say, "Forget science and math; he's going to be queer so just teach him how to put grommets in chaps and get him going with musicals. Here, start him off with *Baker Street.*"

UNCLE JOEL

I have two close friends, Karla and Marshall, for whom I was best man at their wedding. They have two boys who call me Uncle Joel. When they were born, the parents, no dummies, named their lawyer friend, Ray, as godfather. After all, should something happen to them, the kids needed to be provided for, and at the time I was a making a frivolous living touring towns like Toast, Opp, and Bugg Ridge doing children's theater. They did name the younger one Joel, though, and despite being told they just liked the name, I have egomaniacally decided it was in my honor. The older son, Daniel, is now 18, which makes me feel like some patriarchal Old Testament character. I spoke with Daniel on the phone the other day, and he had concerns about going to the senior prom. Good grief. I remembered double-dating with his parents to my prom. Did the biblical patriarchs go through this?

Somehow I seem to have become the "cool" uncle. My job in radio comedy syndication keeps me abreast of all the new music, so I'm able to converse intelligently about this week's hot new band. Make that "knowledgeably" as opposed to "intelligently" because, let's face it, there's not a lot of intelligence involved in pop culture. Since I live in Los Angeles and Daniel is in Delaware, this week's artist here is usually the in-two-to-three-months' artist there. This makes me way cool because he gets alerted to what's coming down the rock music radio pike and is able to stay ahead of the Delaware curve. Because I know who the Propellerheads,

Chemical Brothers and Godsmack are, it logically followed
that Daniel would view me as a source for his other questions
and issues ranging from getting tattoos to moving in with his
ex-girlfriend and her baby (not his) just to get out of the
house, to highly intimate sexual information. This must be
how Dr. Laura, who is a doctor of physiology, thank you, got
her national radio show dispensing psychological advice.
When her callers have something wrong with their physiology, say a bowel obstruction, do they consult a psychiatrist?
But hey, at least it's somebody to talk to, and Daniel had sex
stuff going on that no parent wants to hear from their kid.

In that phone call he asked me how to effect a certain
sexual procedure. While no Lothario, I have, nevertheless,
been around. I started with girls too. I just wasn't very enthusiastic about it. His, then, was a question I could answer. My
problem was, Should I? There was no way in hell he was
going to ask Mom or Dad without having an EMT crew on
the scene, and if I didn't tell him, he was just going to fumble
around, possibly making matters worse and definitely wasting valuable male-peak-of-sex time. Lord knows mine was
wasted taking Penny Pridemore to the prom on a double date
with Daniel's parents and then coming home and beating off
to the men in the *Playboy* "Year In Cinema" issue. What I
wouldn't have given for someone to tell me I should take my
summer stock theater pals up on their tantalizing offers, invitations I shrank from out of fear. That would have helped me
figure things out about myself years earlier.

So I told him.

Now I'm the coolest guy on the planet not currently in a
rock band. At one point Daniel even said I was a role model.
Oy gevalt! If his parents ever hear that, they will board a
plane, fly out here, and my body will not be found. I made a
living working in theater, for crying out loud. I lived in group
houses until I was 30. I shared a one-room apartment with
three people while temping in New York by day and doing

brilliantly scathing if unappreciated satirical revues at night. For most of my life I could fit all my belongings in my dad's old army duffel bag. If I needed to move, I didn't call U-Haul, I called Yellow Cab. I moved to Washington, D.C., when my patchy theater gigs ran out, to New York on a pauper's whim, and then to Los Angeles with no job, no credit, no car, no license, no place to live, and only $500 and a sofa where I could crash. I pretty much fell from temp jobs to make-do stints while writing until, with Fred's pushing and help, I found a position that paid me to do what I've always done for nothing: be silly. This is hardly the résumé Marshall or Karla would wish for Daniel. As far as they are concerned this is a curriculum vitae that does not bear the Good Housekeeping Seal of Approval but rather the Mark of the Beast. Mine is the Antirésumé.

I don't need the pressures of being a role model, anyway. It sounds so mature and responsible. It makes me feel I should be cleaning the house, getting the *Utne Reader,* and increasing my 401(k) withholding. Still, if I can provide a safe place for him when he needs to get something off his chest, I'm happy to do it. He's a good kid and he comes from good parenting, so all the hard work has already been done. Besides, I'm sure he's intelligent enough to pick out the really smart and important things, such as "be who you are" and "moisturize," while forgetting about the dumb stuff I've done like buying a time-share as an investment and the sinking-the-row-boat-in-the-hotel-pool-while-naked incident. And for all my hand wringing, if he wants to make me a role model, there's really nothing I can do about it.

Cool Uncle Joel. The role model. Sheesh.

I'm calling personnel tomorrow and upping my 401(k).

HIGH-TECH TROUBLE
(Off-line, Online, and Out of Line)

I do not enjoy an easy relationship with machines. I have never found them to be logical. They are contrary, fickle, prone not to work at all one day, intermittently the next, and perfectly, of course, any time I try to demonstrate the problem to someone else. They usually also have maddening personalities that do not complement mine. I accept this. There are some people with whom I don't get along. One of our two cats doesn't care for me. But why is it that I have such unhealthy relationships with *all* the machines in my life?

I have a toaster that does not like me. Weeks go by with perfect toast until I get down to the last two slices in the house. Then the toaster burns them. Fred can put the last two slices in and they come out fine. It's only when I do it that they come out blackened. For a while I outsmarted the toaster by waking Fred up and making him put the last slices in for me. The toaster caught on to that, though. I've learned that Fred has to stand there and make the toaster think the toast is for him or it will still burn the bread. My therapist tells me I'm the only one he knows who has issues with a toaster.

I've also had a difficult time with my coffeemaker. If I put the water and coffee in it the night before and set it to brew at 5 A.M., I would get up at 5:15 to find steaming coffee all over the counter and dripping down the cabinets. It did this every time I set it to brew before 7. Only I could buy a coffeemaker that doesn't like to get up early. But I'm not about to be stymied by a Mr. Coffee, so I developed a cunning plan: I set the clock on the coffee maker two hours *ahead* so it would think it was in, say, Chicago. Now I get up at 5:15 to perfectly brewed coffee because my coffeemaker started brewing at 5 because I've rigged its clock to tell it it's 7. I have a relationship with my coffeemaker based on a lie. Worse than that, in fiddling with its clock I've made it lie to itself. I start the day feeling dirty.

Moving to the living room, our VCR gives me attitude. Fred can make it record signals from Tehran at the press of a button. I wrestle with the manual for 20 minutes so I can tell the VCR very carefully exactly what I want it to do and it still does whatever the hell it wants or, often, nothing. Sometimes it does what I asked—only wrong—for instance, without sound. Why would a VCR think I'd want to watch a picture with no sound? No modern machine is that stupid. This is deliberate malice. Just looking at it ticks me off so much I can't even enjoy my porno.

I admit I'm among the least competent people around when it comes to anything remotely technical, but it's not always my fault. Some time ago I dialed the machine at 977-FILM to get the show times for a movie playing at a revival house. The voice program told me to use my Touch-Tone pad to enter the name of the movie I wanted to see. It was Fellini's *8½*. How the hell do you enter that? After four tries I went bowling.

Of all the machines in my life, though, the one that most upsets me is the computer I use at my workplace. My company handles major national radio personalities, but I work on a glamourless product in a rinky-dink corner known to no one. Guess who gets the good computers. The one I had came over on the Mayflower. One time after hours I was feeling randy so I locked my door and surfed the Net for dirty pictures. By the time the first one downloaded, I was done and wanted a sandwich. After much groveling and a public hissy fit people are still talking about, I was finally given a newer computer that used to belong to a producer of the Michael Reagan radio show. I had high hopes that this computer would like me because, being a Democrat, I was more permissive. How was I to know my young and impressionable CPU had been programmed, literally, with right-wing Republican cant? In less than a week it could tell I was a leftist pinko fairy, and it started crashing on me every other day. Sometimes while I'm doing normal inputting, out of the blue it gives me an error message: "This program has performed an illegal operation and will be shut down." This is disturbing on two levels. First, it drives me crazy that it pretends to give me a choice by presenting me with "OK" and "Ignore" buttons. It's not really a choice. I've clicked on "Ignore." It doesn't mean I can ignore the message; it means the machine is going to ignore me until I click on "OK." So I click "OK" because, yeah, I'm OK with losing my work as well as another ten minutes waiting for my computer to reboot. Secondly, I'm upset because when I go through this I feel I am enabling it to commit other illegal operations by not punishing it for this one. After all, silence is tacit agreement, so it's just never going to learn. I know my little computer didn't turn out like I'd hoped, but it's still mine and I care for it.

It has started doing other things too. It doesn't notify me when I have E-mail. If I had a child who habitually hid my mail, I'd consult a child psychologist, but what can I do with a box everyone tells me is a machine following a logical program? And how logical can it be when it stops printing in the middle of a document to tell me the printer parameters are no longer acceptable? The parameters were just fine when it started printing, thank you. I think this is "acting out" behavior because I'm not printing Reaganesque blather about women staying home, gays ruining marriage for heterosexuals, or "my good friend Bob Dornan." I'm not giving it what it wants so it throws a printer tantrum. I have to cancel out of the print queue and resend current page after current page until the document's done. This is an obvious and heartbreaking cry for attention. I've tried spending more time with the machine after hours by telecommuting from home, but I guess there's just no substitute for being there. I feel like a failure.

Now the darned thing is out-and-out lying to me. Every six minutes it says it's autosaving. When I get the inevitable "illegal operation" message and have to reboot, I find nothing has been saved since I last closed whatever document I've been working on. Am I wrong for thinking there are deep issues of trust at stake here?

I'm at my wit's end. I bet the Michael Reagan people knew how to keep it operating properly. The whole thing has made me rethink my politics. Maybe we do need a fascistic oligarchy to keep these machines in line and online. I've mollycoddled it. It lies, it hides things from me, and it's out doing illegal things without my knowledge. I let it go out on the Net to God-knows-where, downloading who knows what kind of virus. I don't even know what sordid illegal operations it's performing; I just pray that whatever it is, it's wearing a condom.

ATHLETICALLY CHALLENGED—
Confessions of a Try-Athlete

Every so often I forget I'm gay and attempt some sport. I know there are plenty of gays who are great athletes, but not me. This is an area where I do not merely fall into the stereotype, I do a double somersault–back flip–belly flop into it.

In college, requirements for my BFA degree made me take gymnastics. The parallel bars hurt my shoulders, the rings and horizontal bar were a joke, and the pommel horse was the scene of a groin injury so traumatic even the teacher referred to that apparatus as "the nutcracker." After that I gravitated to the women's gymnastic events. I even took my final on the balance beam. The only way I could have made more girly gymnastic choices would have been if the Olympics had come up with that Ribbon On a Stick event earlier.

I was also required to take beginning ballet. Believe me, if you're a klutz, ballet is a sport. It's played in embarrassingly revealing tights and a T-shirt in front of a mirror with a room full of lithe, gazelle-like women and maybe two other guys too mortified to look at each other. If you can quit the playing field with any shred of dignity intact, you've won. With my then 250-plus pounds crammed into a large-size dance belt ("No, we do not make extra-large"), I lost. I hated lumbering across the floor in a hopeless pas de chat. I could fall over doing simple pliés. Things were easier in modern dance. If I tripped over my own feet in that class, all I had to do when I hit the floor was hold the pose and it counted as choreography.

Work toward my arts degree also required me to take fencing, which I rather liked because it was simultaneously dashing, elitist, and butch. I also enjoyed putting on other guys' sweaty face masks. I also got off on strapping myself into a somewhat restrictive suit with a crotch flap and buckle that went between my legs. I was rotten at the actual fencing, but what good does it do you even if you're great? Recounting your dramatic flèche and riposte does not rank up there with catching the winning touchdown pass. I didn't care if I sucked at fencing. I compensated by keeping that buckle ni-i-ice and tight.

In later years I tried horseback riding—once. It was like my first time at a sex club, only it smelled better. Interestingly, I was sore afterward in exactly the same places.

I have a golf freak friend named Marshall who can't understand why everyone doesn't want to wear ugly pants and whack balls with a stick. He dragged me out with him once to show me the beauty of the game. It was hot, and I didn't have any sunblock for my balding head. He was rhapsodizing about the vagaries of loft, carbon clubs, and Zen, and all I could think was "I want a mai tai and a hat." I think that was about the third hole. By the time we were done I came away with an utter loathing for golf and mild sun poisoning.

My friend Kevin wants to take me snow skiing but I know better. Skiing is a Bavarian word for "leg breaking." The only part of snow skiing that interests me is the après-ski part with the cocoa and the hot tub and the high jinks of Colt Films' *The Other Side of Aspen.*

Some years ago in North Carolina, my buddies Becky and Scott invited me to go out with them on the Intracoastal Waterway in their father's boat. My idea of boating is to sit back and let the wind blow through the hair on my head, shoulders, and back while sipping an iced tea, maybe find a nice shaded spot and do a little fishing. I saw boating as a chance to do on water what I love to do on land, sit around. Becky and Scott were handsome, strapping, fit, active, youthful siblings, and they were going to teach me how to water-ski. Scott plunged into the water as his sister tossed him the tow rope. She positioned the boat, Scott waved, and Becky gunned it. Naturally Scott came right up like a pro. He slalomed back and forth over the wake of the speeding boat with ease and grace, the wind pressing his baggies against his tantalizingly full crotch. Next up was Becky, and it was the same with her—except for that crotch part. She skied like something out of a Go-Go's video. She got back in the boat and they both looked at me. "OK," I said hopefully, "who wants lunch?" No such luck.

Chafing in a life jacket, I bobbed in the salty water, trying not to lose the tow rope and struggling to position my skis properly, whatever that meant. How hard could this be? Becky and Scott did it, and they were from Montana, for crying out loud. "What's to ski on in Montana?" I thought. I waved my arm, and the boat took off. I was immediately yanked face forward into the water and dragged a quarter mile, mouth wide open in shock and gathering krill. Nobody had bothered to tell me to let go if that happened so, terrified, I hung on for dear life forming a six-foot bubble going down the Intracoastal Waterway. This lasted less than a minute but long enough for me to gulp enough salt water to have me passing sea monkeys for days. Scott killed the engine as soon as Becky shouted I was down. They came around to see if I was OK. That was when I realized my bathing suit was around my right ankle, stopped by the one ski I had managed to retain.

I received more instruction and, with subsequent attempts, more seawater. I managed to get halfway up a couple of times, but either I was too heavy or the boat wasn't going fast enough. My impression of water skiing is that it's a 30-mile-an-hour enema. Becky said I should look on it as a learning experience. So I did. I learned I was as awkward in the water as on land.

These days the most I can muster is occasionally going roller skating on Sunday and Thursday—gay nights at Moonlight Rollerway in Glendale. You lace up your skates and link up with a friend to dish everyone else out on the floor. Or you can sit on the sidelines and watch dozens of gay men skate past. It's a grand parade of rolling homos, and you get to watch your favorites come around again and again. The exercise I get is in choosing one guy, then struggling to stay close behind him so I can watch his butt.

I don't know if I'll get involved in any other athletic activities, but if I do, they'll be a lot like skating at the roller rink. It's fun because it involves gossip with friends and an element of sex, and it doesn't feel like exercise. Besides, where else can you work out, then get a chili dog, cheese nachos, and a snow cone?

MOTHER, MY MOTHER

While I was going through puberty, my mother was going through menopause. Our little house on Sioux Court was hormone hell. I remember one argument in particular. We were yelling in each other's faces as only families can. I had driven her to such distraction she finally shouted, "You son of a *bitch*!" I gasped. Then I cackled and pointed. For a split second she was enraged, then she realized what she'd said and we both howled. Somehow we got through all that plus, years later, my being a homo. "Is Joel gay?" she asked my brother, Brian, who rolled his eyes. Brian told me this, so I went to her and said yes, that was the case. It was why I had been living with Fred for 11 years at the time, why I loved going shopping with her, why I knew every Sondheim musical by heart, and why I was able to help her mix and match her wardrobe *every single time I came back for Christmas*. She thought for a while and I could see her putting the grandchildren dream back in a box. "Oh, honey," she said, placing a sad hand on mine, "and you're not even a good dancer."

Mom always possessed a knack for getting her way. A man named Paul Sylvester, who happened to be the county D.A., lived behind us. He built a kennel for his dogs right next to our property, and this irked my mother to no end. She didn't like the dogs because they were stupid and barked at everything. When she told this to Mr. Sylvester he pooh-poohed her and told her if they barked, she was free to call him any time and complain. Mom narrowed her eyes and said, "You're on." That afternoon Mom bought a Japanese wind chime for 79 cents. She hung it from a tree in our yard right next to the kennel and sat up with a book in the den that evening, waiting. Around 10:30 Mr. Sylvester put the dogs in the kennel and, judging by the bedroom light going off, turned in. Soon a breeze came by, and the delicate chimes tinkled, driving the silly dogs bonkers. Mom calmly dialed Mr. Sylvester's phone. "Paul, your damn dogs are barking." Mr. Sylvester could be heard going out to the kennel where, jerk that he was, he beat the dogs with a rolled up newspaper until they shut up. Then he went back to bed. Mom continued reading her Agatha Christie. Another breeze, another round of barking, another phone call from Mom. Mr. Sylvester went back out to the kennel and beat the dogs. It went on like this all night. Tinkle, tinkle. Bark bark bark. Ring. "Paul, your damn dogs are at it again." Whap whap whap whap. The county D.A. was losing sleep and cases. After three nights of this, both the kennel and the dogs were gone. The wind chimes remained in the tree until we moved years later. Every time they tinkled, Mom smiled.

When I was 9, Nipper Wigmore, who was my age and a natural bully, lived next door. His father, Bus, was a coach at the junior high across the street, so all his boys (Nipper, Skipper, and Andy) had been steeped in manly-man sports. Nipper ostensibly tried to teach me how to hit a baseball—a futile endeavor, as I was to grow up to be gay and care nothing for sports, only for the athletes. I mean, when I think of Mark McGwire and Sammy Sosa I don't think *home runs;* I think *sandwich.* Anyway, Nipper's real intent was to belittle me with hateful taunts until I cried because he knew I was bat-blind and scared of the ball. I swung the bat, missing every single time in my red-faced fury. He pitched to me again and again, coming closer and closer, each time hurling epithets along with the baseball. "You are so stupid!" he bellowed in my quivering, wet face, having achieved his goal.

"How can you be such a fat stupid sissy, you crybaby retard!" I snapped. With one downward arc of the bat, I laid Nipper out cold on his father's prized Bermuda-grass lawn. His mother, Peg, came swooping out of the house, which was no mean feat. Peg Wigmore was what we today tactfully call a "plus size." (On an earlier occasion, my brother and I got into trouble during a neighborhood game of hide-and-seek when we both hid behind her—successfully.) Ignoring her son facedown in the Bermuda, Peg grabbed me by the scruff of the neck, dragged me over to our front door, and beat on it with her lardy fist. My mother opened the door to a seething Peg. "Your Joel just hit my Nipper with a baseball bat!" Mom took my collar and drew me inside with an ominous "I'll handle this" and slowly shut the door on Peg. She marched me over to the living room sofa, the one we were never ever supposed to sit on, and plopped me down. "I saw the whole thing," she said with her hands on her hips, pausing for proper effect. "What the hell took you so long?" I was stupefied. "Get your brother and get in the car." Mom took us to Dairy Queen and afterward, as a special treat, we went to the park and fed the ducks.

Another time I had been allowed to go with Mrs. Jarmen and my friend David, her son who was in my fourth grade class, to watch his brother play Little League Baseball. I could stomach the Little League because I was in love with David, mainly because he treated me nicely. I was also smitten with Mrs. Jarmen because she actually cooked breakfast and didn't mind me showing up for it every day. While waiting for the game to begin, David and I went to the nearby swings where we went so high we could feel the chains snap taut when we swung down. I jumped out of the swing at the bottom of the arc, took one step, tripped over a tree root, and broke my left arm spectacularly. I knew I had done real damage because Mrs. Jarmen made me sit up front as she drove me back home like a maniac, weeping in guilt and terror of what my mother would say. Mom, who was chatting with Peg in the Wigmores' driveway, saw Mrs. Jarmen's car lurch into the middle of our front yard. Mom had been doing sweaty, strenuous lawn work and looked it. Mrs. Jarmen staggered over, an inarticulate mess of tears and snot. Mom pieced it together that I was hurt, assessed the damage, and got me into her car. Then she went inside. What was she doing? Why weren't we going to the doctor? Peg took Mrs. Jarmen into her house to calm her down, and I was left by myself. My arm was huge and throbbing, and nobody was there. Finally Mom came out looking like a million bucks. She had taken a shower and was dressed like she was going to a dinner party with Daddy. The pain was making me nauseous, and I was scared, but this upset me more. When we got to the emergency room, Mom walked in like Cleopatra pissed off at Antony. "Where is Dr. Gleitz?" she demanded in a voice so loud it made fillings ache. The head nurse said he wasn't on call that day, and anyway, we had to fill out emergency room forms. Mom snatched the forms, tossed them in the trash, and strode past the nurse, calling into the corridor, "Where is Dr. Gleitz?" He came in on cue, taking off his coat and putting on his white smock. He whizzed us past the man who had something sticking through his leg and the girl who had been kicked by a horse and led us directly into the X-ray room.

It was years before I understood that the entire time Mom had been in the house she had been on the phone arranging for our family doctor to meet us at the hospital. Meanwhile, cord stretched to its limit, she had taken a shower with the phone to her ear and put on stockings and a dress. The result was that she looked so damn hot when we descended on the emergency room that she was able to command respect and, with the fight of a tiger, walk right over injured others. I cherish—and still use—the two lessons I learned from this: (a) always dress better than your competition and (b) walk in like it's the set of *The Prince of Tides* and your name is Barbra.

These days things are a little more quiet with Mom. She's fighting Alzheimer's tooth and nail, and my Dad is right there helping her do it. Last summer her pet cat died, and she's been wanting another one. My father has resisted because since his heart attack he doesn't have the energy to feed the front end of the cat nor tend a litter box for the back end. Daddy is very religious, much more so than my mother ever was, and she knows it. Last fall she took to telling him in defiant tones, "Douglas, I'm gonna pray for a cat." My father begged her not to do that because he knows prayers are answered. In December I went to visit them. While I was there a gray cat who lives down the street adopted my parents as a second home. He turns up every day or so to come inside, be petted, sit on her lap, and sleep. He leaves when it's time to take care of either of the ends my father so dislikes. Daddy puts it down to the power of prayer—his mitigating hers—but I suspect Mom put food outside. Even now, with the ordeal of the medications and the indignities of Alzheimer's, Mom has a knack for getting her way.

A LITTLE LEARNING

The occasion of my birthday this month has caused me to wonder what, if anything, I've learned in 44 years on the planet. One thing I've learned is that I'm no expert on life. Something else I've learned is that not being an expert has never stopped me from running off at the mouth. So here are a few of the things I've picked up along the way:

Some of us are "show-ers" and some of us are "growers." "Show-ers" who grow piss me off.

Always weigh yourself with your shoes on. That way you can mentally deduct the estimated weight of your footwear. My shoes currently weigh 25 pounds.

A mind is a perfectly good thing to waste—take it to the beach and give it a Jackie Collins novel.

Food costs more in direct proportion to its proximity to over-roasted coffee. The same muffin that's 45 cents at the grocery is a buck fifty at the diner and $3.95 at Starbucks.

I don't care what the copy says, straight men do not advertise in the personals sections of gay magazines. Also, anyone advertising that they are "straight acting" has a problem with being gay. Who wants to get in bed with that?

Never lean against a washroom counter. Especially in unlined pants. Also, do not choose a hot day to go without underwear in light khakis.

Magazines like *Interview* go to parties and take pictures of total nobodies. Then they print them to make us think they're way cooler than we are because we don't know who the hell these pasty pockmarked people are. "Roger Bell-Escovel and Lisa Q show their fashion savvy, bad teeth, and track marks at SoHo's new Club Cloaca." Golly, *Interview* must be cutting-edge because these are such the happening hipsters. Here I thought they looked like psychiatric patients just wandering in to mix vodka with Zoloft.

French passive is not a verb tense. And call me a pushy bottom, but Greek active means active, so hop to it! Sir.

Everyone thinks Alex Trebek is so smart. Wake up, people, they give him the answers.

Gay porn stars should stop being so coy with their thinly veiled sexual screen names like Peter Wilder or Carl Hardwick and just go all the way. I want to see a porno tape starring Dick Party.

Travel expands the mind but wrecks the colon.

Parking Enforcement officers are evil and will all be assigned to a particularly nasty ring of hell. Oh, and you can write them checks for "35 fucking dollars and zero fuck-you cents." It still comes out of your account, but getting that canceled check back is a lot more satisfying.

Good looking is not enough. That's a big one. (Come to think of it, a big one is not enough either.)

I have questions too, which I ponder. For instance, if time flies when you're having fun, do you age faster at Disneyland? Why do banks lend millions to unstable countries but hassle me over a $20 check? Why is it that the Marines produce the best bottoms? How does 15 minutes of fame translate into a two-hour TV movie?

Getting older means I inherit the right to be cranky about things I don't like. For instance, what is this thing with the tip jar at a coffee counter? I urged my congressperson to raise the minimum wage specifically so I would not have to tip the surly nihilistic kid handing me coffee in a paper cup for which I had to spend 20 minutes in line. You want a tip? Come to my table, take my order, bring it to me, and, for crying out loud, flirt. Damn it, it's called service! While we're at the coffee counter, this once I will give you a tip: Knock it off with the nihilist crap. You're 20, for crying out loud; you should be having sex five times a night. With caffeine, eight times a night. *That* is a reason to get up in the morning, OK?

All right, enough with the cranky. Here are some things I really like. Cops on bicycles—who knew Kevlar could be so sexy? Gelato—yet another reason to seek out Italians and express extremely personal thanks. Construction crews in summer—they may not all look like Lucky Vanous, but they're just as sweaty and twice as real. Indirect lighting—I'm appreciating this more with every passing year.

I like seeing Humvees in the city. When a person is so unstable they need a car the size of the Castro to make up for being hung like a Tic-Tac, it's good to have something as obvious as a Humvee to warn the rest of us.

I like Christopher Lowell, the host of *Interior Motives,* a home-decorating show on cable. He's a big ol' homo, girlfriend, nancy-boy decorator and I absolutely love him for it. One day on the show he was visiting an equally obvious friend who had put in fabulous plants around his pool. While Christopher was chatting to us about bromeliads, the friend blatantly cruised Chris on camera for all to see. They don't call it the Discovery Channel for nothing.

Which brings me back to the subject of what I've discovered in this life, so, in no particular order, here's the rest of it:

"One size fits all" is a lie.

No one goes to the gym to compensate for being too smart.

There is nothing festive about festival seating.

You know you are friends when you can discuss dingleberries over dinner.

I absolutely believe it's not butter.

Dating someone over 35 does not qualify as a charity event.

Only people with three hands should be allowed car phones.

And "Must See TV" isn't.

The number one thing I've learned, though, is that compared to all I don't know, what I've learned thus far is a paltry list indeed. I look forward to the remaining time I have in hopes of learning a few more things like, oh, patience, forgiveness, and wisdom. In the meantime, I'm going to go learn what triple-chocolate velvet cake tastes like when spoon-fed to me by my honey in bed. We have to muss the sheets first, so I'll end by saying two things. Firstly, here's to another year of life in all its upsetting, ecstatic, thrilling, unpredictable, crazy-making glory. Secondly, send all cards, gifts and cash care of my publisher.

Let me emphasize the cash. If I've learned anything, it's that money goes with everything.

PART TWO
Story Time I

CLOTHES ENCOUNTERS

Recently my friend Greg took me to a bar. He didn't tell me where we were going, so I hopped in his car not bothering to change out of my khaki Dockers, button-down flower-print Gap shirt, and Top-Siders. We went to the Gauntlet, Los Angeles's premiere hard-core leather bar.

I had never been there, and in that outfit I felt like Martha Stewart in a mosh pit. I wanted to kill my friend but he had already attached himself—literally—to a man wearing what appeared to be an entire set of tire chains. I realized that only a week earlier I had ended up in something very like that while attempting to assemble my nephew's swing set. My friend was led away, and I was left to blend in by myself. "Bartender, a double anything."

I enjoy being exposed to new things, which turned out well because there were many patrons who enjoyed exposing their things. I suppose if you go to the pain and expense of having something pierced five or six times, you'd want somewhere you could show it off, tie it back, or lace it up, and this was the place. Body parts it has never occurred to me to stretch—except in angry fantasies concerning my boss—not only had been stretched but were being displayed. The thought came to me that, should I run into my boss there, I could act on my violent impulses and be doing him a favor. I decided to stroll.

I was having a good time taking in the sights, but I couldn't help wondering how one strikes up a conversation in a place like this. I saw a man come in wearing leather chaps with the butt cut out, a green rubber shirt, and elbow-length sewer gloves. What do you say to that? "Oh, thank God, I almost wore the same thing"? Everywhere I turned I was confounded by what to talk about. I kept trying to come up with opening chitchat but everything seemed wrong. "Did you manage that yourself or did you have to get someone to tie you into it?" "Golly, where do they sell jodhpurs?" "Hi there, nice leash!" "Can you get that at the Men's Wearhouse, or is Gestapo wear catalog only?" "Jeepers, when you had that done, did you black out?"

Dressed like a big vanilla preppy twit, I was getting only well-deserved sneers anyway. I despaired of finding anyone willing to talk to me in my outfit. My hopes rose when I saw a guy wearing only construction boots and briefs. I thought "All right! I can look like I belong here if I just strip!" Then I remembered my underwear was a pair of Yogi Bear and Boo-Boo boxers with red hearts my lover had given me for Valentine's Day. Damn. I thought back to the man in the tire chains and wondered if I couldn't go back to the car and whip up something with floor mats.

Soon I realized I was wasting my time even considering conversation. If you weren't the bartender, nobody talked to you. It was all attitude and getting your point across with surly looks and macho gestures. I can do that. I studied mime.

So I decided to ignore what I was wearing and play the game. I adopted the go-to-hell stance and waited for a response. After a while a man with a thick chain running from nipple to nipple and down to something in his leather hot pants sneered at me. I sneered back. He crossed the room like he was going to kick in my ribs with his biker boots and grabbed my print shirt with a low grunt. "Oh, what foul, disgusting sex talk is he going to spew?" I thought in eager, nay, breathless anticipation. He looked derisively at my shirt. "Gap," he growled, "$12.99 on sale." That pissed me off because nothing hurts like the truth. Well, almost nothing, as I discovered. I grabbed his chain and yanked. He doubled over. Apparently the lower extension was anchored in a place and fashion I had not anticipated, and my action had an undesired effect. That being: Pain was good, and he wasn't going to leave me alone the rest of the evening.

Other than the relationship I have with my parents, I haven't explored S/M, so I had no idea how to get rid of my masochist in short shorts. And I did want to be rid of him, especially after he told me what I paid for my pants, which I'd recently purchased on sale at Robinsons-May. Who knew it was *The Price Is Right* night at the Gauntlet? I snorted and walked away. He followed. I insulted him, but that only made matters worse. I needed time to think, so I ordered him to lick my shoes. Instantly he dropped to his hands and knees as I desperately tried to remember anything I could from *Black and Blue,* a video I had rented believing, mistakenly, it would feature African-American policemen. Suddenly he was back in my face. "What the hell is this?" he demanded, "You're wearing Top-Siders."

"Yes, and I got them at an outlet in Maine," I snapped, "so go on, tell me what I paid." Vaguely I started to remember a scene from the video and felt inspired. "Guess correctly and I'll drip hot wax, um..." the image faded, "...someplace *really* tender."

He looked at me like I was a bug. Then: "$49.95."

"Ha! $35, and they threw in extra laces and a shoe care kit!"

"You're a freak," he said, adjusting the chains in his giant tit rings. He walked away looking back over his shoulder at me to toss off a final sneer as he bumped smack into a large man dressed like a Mountie who threatened to punch him out. Ah, *l'amour!*

I was happy for my freewheeling fetishist, but I wanted out of there. I was raised to dress for the occasion, and I felt sure this was only the latest in the many ways I was letting my parents down. Luckily, I saw my friend Greg at the bar. He and Mr. Tire Chains had found a USC student and a dark corner. They were going about their business avidly when college boy got his braces caught in a couple of links and the spark had gone out of the evening. It hadn't been a total loss for Greg, though, as he'd somehow had acquired a set of regulation handcuffs. The bad news was, there was no key; the good news was, the cuffs were only on one of his hands, so he wasn't going to have to teach me how to drive his manual transmission to get home. We toasted the fact he had two days to get them off before work on Monday, tipped the bartender, who sneered his appreciation, and left.

As I prepared for bed, I reflected that there must have been a convention of peace officers in town because there seemed to be so very many cops at the Gauntlet that night. It was good to see them and know nothing untoward would be going on there. Especially because I wanted to go back. And next time I'd be dressed.

MY NIGHT OF 1,000, OK, THREE, MAYBE FOUR CELEBRITIES

I love living in Los Angeles, if only for the celebrity sightings: Mickey Dolenz in Thrifty Drug buying cheap Valentines, Diana Ross in Payless selecting a douche, Sally Struthers in Gelson's at the salad bar—at least that's what I think was behind her, it was hard to tell. I've even had the occasional twofers: Goldie and Kurt wearing please-don't-recognize-us sunglasses *inside* the Laemmle Royal movie theater, Ellen and Anne being overt with french fries in the *trés* trendy eatery Red on Beverly. Sure, we see them, but do they even notice us? I had occasion recently to be well remembered by three, possibly four celebrities.

Fred and I began our evening out at Book Soup Bistro on Sunset. I saw a distinguished older man at the bar noticeable for his white silk pants and brown and white coat that perfectly matched his suede saddleback shoes. I am of the opinion that nobody over the age of 30 can get away with saddlebacks, but here was a man who never got the memo. Suddenly we heard an unmistakable basso profundo voice call out, "Gene, how are you!" James Earl Jones, looking every bit as magnificent as he sounds, greeted the man, and they chatted. Mr. Jones introduced the handsome woman with him, whom I can only assume was Mrs. Jones. After pleasantries, "Gene" shook hands and excused himself, and the Joneses were seated at a table beside us. All we could do was try not to giggle from hearing the exquisitely enunciated, barrel-deep voice of Darth Vader saying things like, "Would you like a roll, my dear?" It sounded like an ex–Jedi knight winding down after a good day of destroying rebel planets. He had the chicken, and I kept expecting to hear, "Luke, give yourself over to the dark meat." Fred and I were crying from unforgivably immature laughter, so much so that he knocked a spoon to the floor. Every time the Joneses glared at us, it just made matters worse to the point I had to go pee. As I got up I stepped on the spoon, twisted my ankle, and knocked into their table, sending a forkful of chicken in cream sauce down Mrs. Jones's front. While I babbled apologies, Fred threw down what I hoped was enough cash, took me by the arm, and got me out of there.

We had reservations for a show at the Tiffany Theater, and we arrived later than planned. There was a crowd already in the lobby, spilling onto the sidewalk. It was cold, so after picking up our tickets I shouldered my way inside to wait. I had just realized this grouping was actually a line when I accidentally stepped on a man's foot. He rightfully and very loudly complained about clumsy line-cutters as I apologized. Moving away, I recognized him as the man who played LeBeau on *Hogan's Heroes*. I returned to Fred utterly starstruck.

"I just stepped on Robert Clary! Isn't that amazing?"

"Not really," Fred said. "He's very short."

Once in our seats, Fred pointed out Bea Arthur wearing a beautiful bright red wool jacket and settling into her seat. Not a minute later we saw Mr. Saddleback Shoes come in, kiss her, and take the seat next to her. I grabbed Fred's arm. "He's Bea Arthur's husband! That's Gene Saks!"

"Who?"

"The Broadway director. *Barefoot in the Park, The Odd Couple*?" Fred stared blankly at me. "*Mame,* for crying out loud. What kind of a homo are you?"

"Did he do the movie too?"

"Did *Mame* suck horse turds?"

Fred elbowed me, and I saw Bea giving me the coldest of stares. I have got to learn to whisper.

"Wait a minute," said Fred, who knows everything about all TV celebrities. "They divorced years ago, and who goes out with their ex? I mean, would you go out with Brad again?"

"Never!" I said. Possibly a lie but still the right answer. The lights dimmed, and the show began. Someone was wearing a perfume that made me rub my nose to keep from sneezing for the entire first act. At intermission I fought the crowd into the men's room to blow my nose. I opened a stall to get tissue. There sat Robert Clary, highly indisposed and most unhappy about the reunion. He spat something in French and I backed out *tout de suite*. I fled the men's room forgetting all about tissue. Then, near the bar, I caught a whiff of that damned perfume and sneezed violently. It was so sudden I was unable to cover my mouth. I landed a hideous phlegm ball on the back of a beautiful bright red wool jacket. I'd hocked a loogie on Bea Arthur! She hadn't noticed, but my upbringing wouldn't allow me to walk away. I got a napkin from the bar and maneuvered around to where she was now standing in a swirl of people. I brushed by, artfully wiping her shoulder blade. Instead of recovering the errant snot, though, I only rubbed it further into the fabric. Aghast, I dabbed again. And again. Bea Arthur whipped around causing my final dab to be at her left breast.

"May I help you?" she growled. I think she growled. Maybe it was just her normal voice.

"I'm sorry," I started to confess, "but I just, I mean, I know you aren't aware of this but I just, um, I..." Confess? What am I, stupid? "I loved *The Golden Girls*."

"Thank you." she said, giving me an icy look that distinctly meant "Go away."

I did. Resuming my seat next to Fred, I told him what had

happened. He shook his head. "I leave you alone for ten minutes," he said, "and you catch LeBeau taking *le dump* and cop a feel from Maude? If I were famous, I'd have a restraining order on you." The lights went down for the second act, which was as loud and dull as the first. When it was over Fred pushed me through a side exit, minimizing all possible sitcom star contact.

We went back to Book Soup Bistro to get the dessert we'd missed earlier and to dish the play. After my second decaf I excused myself to visit the men's room. Passing through the bar, I saw Bea Arthur sipping a martini, with an unattended drink beside her. I wondered who she was there with and nodded as I passed. She narrowed her eyes, no doubt to discourage me from pawing her further.

In the men's room stall next to mine was a pair of saddleback suede shoes with white silk pants around them. Well, at least I hadn't done anything to the debatable Gene Saks. After all, I had knocked food down the front of Darth Vader's wife, seen Robert Clary's *croquettes,* and goobered on a Golden Girl. "It's been quite a night for apologies," I thought to myself, pulling up my pants, "I'm just glad it's over." Then I flushed.

To my horror, instead of the water going down, it rose and continued to rise. The floor drain was in the other stall, and the water was still rising. Silk? Suede? Oh, this was not going to be pretty. There does not exist an apology in the English language sufficient to cover what was about to occur. So, with water spilling down the side of the bowl, I did the only thing anyone could do. I shouted, "Mr. Saks, that's for *Mame*!" and I bolted.

APRIL FOOL'S

Every year we mark the date, but how many of us really know the melancholy yet colorful origins of April Fool's? It started in Germany during the Dark Ages, so called because there were no electric lights. During the annual court festivities held the last day of March at midnight, making it therefore very dark, people bumped into each other—a lot—especially on the dance floor. It so happened one year that wise King Pfefferneuse IV, who was a smart cookie, had a court jester named Apool who was known as quite a dancer, mainly for not bumping into all that many people. Apool made a further name for himself by choreographing moves making sport of people at court such as Gottfried of Fick, notable for weighing over 300 pounds. For him Apool danced the Chunky Ficken. Indeed, he made his master laugh so much that the king granted his fool, Apool, 5,000 Deutsche Marks. This was amazing because, at the time, no one knew there were that many people in Deutschland named Mark.

Apool and the 5,000 Marks lived together sharing household duties. For instance, Mark did the cooking, Mark thatched the roof, Mark hunted game (he was the marksman), Mark did the marketing (especially on days things were marked down), and thus they marked time. It was remarkable, but even I'm getting tired of this. Markedly so.

OK, going on. After about a year of fooling around with these guys—what else would he do?—it became apparent to Apool that he was unable to support them. Although having so many men around was heavenly, he realized he was living in a fool's paradise. He decided to petition the king, but before he could get enough signatures, the king came to Apool saying, "What is it you wish, my jester?" Apool said, "Sire, we are starving." The king said, "In that case, I grant you 10,000 French franks."

The franks were delicious, and Apool and the Marks ate them with relish. The Marks supplied the relish, making the meal a Deutsche treat. But because of the exchange rate (two franks to the Mark) this was only good for one meal. Apool approached the monarch again. "If you truly enjoy my merry frolic," said Apool, "show your pleasure in coin."

"You would fain frolic for filthy lucre?" Pfefferneuse IV frowned forebodingly.

Apool said he didn't mind filthy lucre; he could have it dry-cleaned. "And, sire," he continued, "I must tell you that I am asking for a pretty penny."

"I was thinking of showering you with gold," the King shrugged, "but if it's a nice penny you want..." he said, digging in his pocket.

Apool quickly replied, "No, no, the gold will do nicely."

So Apool gratefully received his golden shower and returned home, where he asked the Marks what he should do with the money. The one who was strongest and therefore a Mark of distinction came forward. He said Apool should use the money to buy more franks. Another Mark, this one from the town of Zorro (relax, I'm not going to say it), declared he was tired of franks and wanted beans. Apool promised a compromise, and that day set off to buy beans and franks. It was a fool's errand, but then all of his errands were.

In the forest he met a bean seller, recognizable by his bright cap with a propeller on top. The bean man came from far-off Kurdistan and also sold tofu. "Hail to you, bean Kurd!" said Apool. "Whence come your fine beans?"

The man claimed to have beans from South America.

"These are from the capital of Peru," he said, displaying them. "They are Lima beans."

But Apool didn't trust any pun that only worked on paper, so he opted for beans from the long skinny country just south of Peru. After Apool got a receipt for the Chile beans, he watched the bean man put the quill pen in his shirt pocket, which held several other pens. The man was obviously a nerd Kurd.

Later that day Apool met a frank seller who told Apool he was ugly because, in addition to being a very frank seller, he was also blunt. That made Apool angry, so he stole the frank frank seller's franks, which was, frankly, easy to do because although he may have been blunt, he wasn't very sharp.

Apool returned home that evening with his beans and franks. He boiled the beans, but since the franks were stolen they were already hot. He then mixed the beans and franks together for a dish he called…legumes and wieners. After Apool and the Marks had all eaten their fill, the Mark of Zorro (OK, I said it, so sue me) announced to Apool that while he had been off filching franks in the forest, the Marks had been practicing a special concert to thank him for his generosity. They immediately broke into beautiful music, singing such songs as "Bean on Me," "Have You Never Bean Mellow?" and Puccini's "O mio babbeano caro."

Apool thought they were marvelous and had a wonderful idea. He would share this gift of song with the king, ending with a solo of his own, either a song about his own generosity ("What Kind Apool Am I") or a statement of his personal creed ("What Apool Believes"), which would have been a Doobie-ous choice. Anyway, he gave the Marks large second helpings of legumes and wieners and while they were eating, he ran to the castle where he begged for an audience with the king. The audience had been sent home earlier, but he was able to see the king alone. "Sire," he entreated, "I want you to come with me!"

"I try," said the king, "but I get too excited."

"No, no, I mean to my house," said Apool.

"Oh," the king said, "that I can do." So they ran off together to Apool's house, where the Marks stood ready to sing.

Now, at dinner Apool had eaten several of the Marks' wieners. If you think I'm going somewhere with that, forget it. The point is, he had not eaten the beans and was therefore unaware of their effect on the Marks, who were stuffed with double servings each of the legumes and wieners.

Apool seated the king directly in front, promising the concert would be a gas. Alas, it was too true, for as the Marks opened their mouths to sing the opening number, "Bean Angel," there came instead a note from behind that was very loud and extremely sour in many ways. The king was so outraged that he caused a major stink, but it was nothing compared to the stink caused by the combined flatulence of the mortified Marks, all of whom fled in flagrant and fragrant embarrassment. "Apool!" wheezed the winded king, "You are fired! Now get me a perfumed handkerchief!" Apool refused because having been fired, he was now nobody's fool. He even flipped the bird, which was a very rude jester. This made the king absolutely livid. "In that case," he fumed among the fumes, "I reclaim all the pieces of gold I gave you only yesterday!"

"Did the king lie when he gave me the gold?" demanded Apool.

"The king does not lie!" he lied, "It was, um, er, a trick! Yes! Ha, ha! And what a funny Pfefferneuse am I! Or actually am IV. But it was all in fun and good spirits, and I hope you starve to death!"

Apool was thenceforth forced to beg for his bread as well as any luncheon meats or condiments he might wish to put on it. Toward the end people wouldn't even give him gum because beggars can't be chewers. In desperation he had WILL FROLIC FOR FOOD tattooed on his foolish forehead, but it was an empty promise, not worth the pauper it was printed on. Poor, poor Apool. He never understood how he had been made incredibly rich and then become a beggar within a single day. Finally he died on the first day of April, which is the sad reason we celebrate April Fool's Day on April 1.

Now, there's nothing like a good story with a moral, and since this is nothing like a good story, you may be sure it has a moral. If you haven't guessed it by now, it is this:

Apool and his money are soon farted.

And by the way, how much did you pay for this book?

WOODWARD, BERNSTEIN, AND WATERGATE

Every time I go to North Carolina I hear some delightfully macabre tale that could only happen there. While visiting my parents in Wilmington a couple of weeks ago, I met my friend Jay at a restaurant downtown. Lounging graciously at the bar, he told me the tale of his mother and her pets in the slowest, most chahmin' drawl y'eveh huhd. I won't inflict further dialect on you, but it'll help to keep it in mind when you read his story:

"Mother was coming back from prayer meeting when she passed a man on the side of the road selling things by a field of collards. Ever alert for a bargain, Mother slammed on the brakes and backed up the quarter mile or so to the man's pickup. Turns out he was selling tires and cockatiels. Lord knows why he was selling those particular items, but there he was. Well, Mother just fell in love with the cockatiels and bought one, along with a tire she was going to turn into a planter for out by the mailbox, but never mind that.

"By the time she got home she had decided to name it Watergate—the cockatiel, not the tire. Mother never did like Nixon, and she already had two miniature dachshunds named Woodward and Bernstein. She hung up the cage in the family room, and there Watergate stayed for several years, the apple of Mother's eye. She gave it free rein in the house, and I would frequently return from visits with unsightly stains on my clothes. Cockatiels display affection by regurgitating, and Watergate was highly taken with me. I did not return his sentiments.

"Anyway, one day Watergate died of no apparent cause. Mother came into the family room, and there he was on the bottom of the cage, little bird legs up in the air, bless his heart. Mother loved Watergate, and this like to tore her to pieces. So she scooped him up, put him in a Tupperware bread box, and stuck him in the freezer. That bird stayed in there for over a year before Mother found someone to stuff him like she wanted. I'd forgotten all about him.

"Then one afternoon I was bringing her some butter beans, and oh, my Lord, there was Watergate hanging on the wall. One wing stretched out in front, the other one reaching round to the rear like he'd been flying through the house, banked into a sharp curve, hit the wall, and stuck. Poor Watergate seemed to look surprised about the whole thing, which I imagine he was. Mother was very happy with him, though. She covered him in Saran Wrap so he wouldn't get dusty, and there he hung, wrapped in plastic, for many months.

"The next spring, Mother was hanging new wallpaper. She took Watergate down, still in Saran Wrap, and set him on the sofa. While she was out back on the porch mixing paste, one of Mother's dogs, Woodward, got hold of Watergate. It wasn't pretty. That dog chewed that poor stuffed bird something fierce, with Bernstein barking like crazy wanting a turn at him too. Mother heard the commotion and ran in. Lord, she was mad. She yanked a knot in both dogs and threw them out of the house. Mother started crying because her dear Watergate was pretty much a loss. She found his head, though, underneath the sideboard, so she went into a closet looking for something in which to keep it as a fond memento.

"Meantime, Woodward was out front busy choking to death on a piece of Saran Wrap. Mother discovered him that evening when she was going out to the car to go play bingo. Bingo is at the *Catholic* church, but Mother can be open-minded where cash prizes are concerned. Anyway, Mother tripped over Woodward in the dark and fell into the camellias, scratching her face something awful. There she was, bloody in her Bingo outfit, and there was Woodward, cold, stiff, and all bug-eyed from choking. Mother wanted to bring him inside, but upon death Woodward had, well, evacuated. So she got the garden hose and sprayed him down. Then she got an extension cord and a blow dryer. When she was done, it was little Woodward's turn in the Tupperware bread box. Next day Mother called the man who'd stuffed Watergate, but he'd been involved in a hunting accident and had gone to his reward. Poor little Bernstein just sits by the refrigerator these days, bless his heart. Mother swears he knows his friend's in there. 'He always was the smart one,' Mother says. 'That's why I gave him the Jew name.'"

"All that was last year. You can go over there today and see Watergate's head in a ring box right there on the TV. Mother did learn her lesson with Saran Wrap, though, so it's displayed under a glass dome. And of course, till she can find another taxidermist, Woodward resides in the freezer to this day. Which is why I am meeting Mother *here* for supper."

Jay took the last sip of his Gibson. "I prefer not to eat over there, knowing what's in the Frigidaire." He shook his head. "I don't know what we'll do if Bernstein goes. Get more Tupperware, I guess."

DEAD MAN FLOATING

Here's a fun fact: Coffins are airtight, so when the ground is saturated, they act like bubbles, rising right out of the ground. Recently, in eastern North Carolina, Hurricane Floyd provided the means for this. Coffins by the dozens rose from cemeteries along the Tar River and were carried away in ghoulish flotillas at the floodwaters' whim.

When Ruby Burgess returned to her soggy house outside tiny Chocowinity, N.C., she found the receding waters had left a pickup truck, numerous uprooted trees, half a dozen dead pigs, and a coffin in her yard. When she examined the coffin she was so shocked she had to sit down on it. She knew this casket—the genuine brass handles with the special spiral metalwork, the wood grain, the decorative plaque the man at the funeral parlor had talked her into. No doubt about it, this was her dearly departed no-good lying bastard husband, dead these 18 months and delivered, yea, even unto her hands. Ruby thanked a vengeful but just God for answering her prayers that the cheating son of a bitch should end up someplace awful. And she knew just where that was.

She found a working phone in town and called her son Earl in nearby Kinston. Earl's lover, Toby Hornack, ran a farm equipment rental place, and Ruby wanted some digging done something awful.

"Momma, Toby's got his hands full right now. He's out driving the wheel-loader himself, helping the Ruperts scoop up their dead pigs."

"I don't need a scooper, I need a digger. Why won't you pay attention?"

"A wheel-loader has a scoop on the front and a backhoe for digging on the rear."

"Perfect. I got dead pigs that need scooping too. We can scoop and then dig. Then we'll have pie, would you like that?"

Two days later, just before dusk, Earl and Toby showed up at Ruby's with the wheel-loader. They were invited to hear how Ruby had survived the hurricane and floods all by herself and utterly alone, but Toby decided he'd rather collect bloating pigs. He left Earl to endure his mother inside. He started the wheel-loader and maneuvered it expertly, gathering swollen hog carcasses with the scoop end and piling them in a stinking heap in a corner of the backyard. Then he doused them with gasoline and set them afire.

"Mercy!" said Ruby, brought to the back screen door by the bright light, black smoke, and hissing fat. "I figured you'd just bury them."

"Gotta burn 'em to stop diseases," Toby told her.

With the pigs out of the way, Ruby decided it was time for the main event. "Earl, honey," she said, "can I show you something in the yard?" She took a gas lantern, led them outside to a pile of brush, and pulled away a large branch. She held up the lantern and said, "Earl, your father's come home."

When they revived Earl, Ruby explained her plan. When her property was incorporated in the city limits a couple of years earlier, she had been forced to hook up to municipal water and sewer. Consequently, the septic tank in her backyard was idle and, as she saw it, the perfect final resting place for Earl's lying-ass, whore-chasing, philandering father.

Earl balked.

"Damn it, Earl, he was seeing That Woman for four years. Have you forgotten how he lied to me? How he shacked up with that bitch? Over *Christmas*?"

Earl crossed his arms, adamant.

Ruby brought out the big guns. "Sweetheart, I never told you why he ran off with That Woman. I think it's time you knew." She touched her son's arm for maximum effect. "He said it was 'cause his only son turned out a prancing, worthless queer, so he had to start over."

Earl reeled against the coffin.

Toby was incensed for his lover. "That fucker," he growled.

Ruby nodded sadly. Her work was done.

Earl stood. "Gimme the keys, Toby."

"You don't know how to operate it, Earl."

"I'll learn."

So, with Toby over his shoulder in the wheel-loader, Earl learned to drive a backhoe. Toby had to take over when they got to the tank in order to break through the concrete top. They were unprepared for the stench. Further difficulty was encountered by the unforeseen fact that septic tanks have a series of walls and screens called baffles that regulate flow. But Ruby, Earl, and Toby were on a mission, and the baffles were beaten down. By the eerie light of burning hogs, the coffin was lifted by the scoop end of the wheel-loader, unceremoniously dumped into years-stagnant, abiding effluvia, and covered over. Back inside the trio shared half an apple pie and a pint of Jack Daniel's Black, then went to bed, each with a fulfilling sense of apt closure.

The next morning, a well-dressed man came to the door. "I'm terribly sorry to have to put you through this, Mrs. Burgess," he said, "but I'm afraid the flood has unearthed several of the caskets from our cemetery. The good news is we've located your late husband's remains."

On the downbeat, three people went, "Oh?"

"Yes. There are numbers on the caskets for this kind of thing. We've identified Mr. Burgess's casket and brought him back. If there are no objections, he'll be reinterred tomorrow. Would you like to attend?"

All three remained frozen. The man wondered if being slow of mind and bug-eyed ran in the family. Ruby was the first to remember to breathe. "No," she said. "We already had our burial."

The man understood and left. Earl and Toby decided they weren't hungry for breakfast after all and took the wheel-loader back to Kinston. Ruby saw them off and went around to the backyard to contemplate a garden where the plants would have access to all the fertilizer they'd ever need. And somewhere near the Tar River there's an innocent person in deep shit.

PART THREE
To Live and Shop in L.A.

SHOPPING FOR CLOTHES—Getting What I Need

I have found a place where the men are all gay, they all look fabulous, and they all want me. It's Bloomingdale's! And think what you will, I know they all want what's in my pants. OK, so it's my Visa card, but I choose to forgive them that, as brazen as they are. And they are brazen. Because they know I will forgive them.

I do love Bloomingdale's. It's so open, bright, pretty, and unnecessary. There is not one thing in Bloomingdale's that you really, truly need. I love that.

I admit I'm being overly rhapsodic, but I haven't been shopping in over six months. I love shopping. They think there may be a gene for being gay. If they ever find it, the gene for shopping will be right next door. The DNA will be structured gay, shopping, Diana Ross. Unless you're a lesbian, in which case it will be gay, shopping for tools, Holly Near. So I adore shopping. And I love buying. It's just that paying thing that gets in the way. God invented shopping; Satan came up with the Visa bill. Or at least my bill. Which is why I haven't allowed myself to go shopping for so long. But after stumbling into Bloomingdale's I can say "Beverly Center...I'm ba-a-ack!"

Even when I was young I loved shopping, but mine was a deprived childhood. I grew up in North Carolina. That's the deprived part. In Wilmington, N.C., we had a Chess King and Sears. There was a Penney's, but it was downtown and catalog only. Mom would bring the catalog home, and I'd flip through it, saying, "Ugh, ugh, ugh, ugh, oh, now that's cute...but look what he's wearing!" I talk about this as if I knew I was gay back then. I had no clue, but I did have taste. Not much, but in Wilmington it doesn't take a lot to get noticed. When I was 10 my father, a Realtor, was getting dozens of keys made in Sears. I was bored out of my skull waiting for him, so I started putting different belts on the mannequins. This gorgon of a saleswoman grabbed me, called the manager, and caused a huge scene. My father came, and they accused me of shoplifting until he pointed out I hadn't taken anything, just switched things around. When we got back to the car, he sat me down and asked, "What on earth made you switch belts?" I burst into post-traumatic stress tears, "They were wrong!" A week later we went back. The mannequins were still wearing my belts.

Other times, Mom would try on things in the dressing room, come out, and ask my opinion. Being gay, it didn't occur to me not to have one. "Well," I'd say, "if you get that hat you're gonna need the brown gloves." Am I dating myself? I was 8. When I was older and I would come home from college or later visit at Christmas, Mom would whisk me to her closet and pull out all the clothes she'd bought while I was away and ask what went with what. And she was surprised when I told her I was gay? If she'd been on the ball, she could have told me. It would have saved me years of confusion, uncertainty, and therapy.

For years shopping was my therapy. There was no upset that could not be calmed by dashing to the mall and buying a new outfit. Of course, the time I did that at the Limited brought on other stress, but that's another story. Now when I'm depressed I no longer go shopping; I see Dr. Finberg for $120 a session. You would not believe the money I'm saving.

Now, of course, I live in Los Angeles, where the shopping is fabulous. I would like to share with you some of my favorite stores. International Male. Rarely go there but love the catalog. I have every one since 1980. Bound. It must be difficult to work there. I can't imagine keeping a straight face while charging 70 bucks for something made of knotted kite string. Turn it one way, it's a shirt; turn it another, it's a thong. Either way it covers exactly nothing. They also sell clothes from the military of foreign nations, countries where they must suffer greatly from feelings of inadequacy because all the pants come with crotch enhancers. Now, that's a government that cares for its military. Hey, wanna look like a pirate? Go to International Male. Although I don't exactly understand the concept. To wear this outfit you have to spend months at the gym getting big, buffed, and butch, an achievement that is totally undone by a frilly shirt that ties in a bow and poofy pants last seen in an M.C. Hammer video. You look about as threatening as Isaac Mizrahi on the Bounty. The other 95% of the clothes there can only be categorized as Cling-Wear. They can be worn only by men who have perfect bodies and the sad need to exhibit them. Clearly these men are struggling with attractiveness issues, and I feel sorry for them. I do. I refuse to believe anyone can look that good and be happy.

Nordstrom. I love that they have a real person playing a real piano. I love that they sell Polo sweatshirts for $109, but coffee is still a quarter. I love that returns are a snap. "I bought these pants yesterday, but this morning I found all these stains." "Oh, dear, did you wear them anywhere?" "Basic Plumbing's Full Moon Sex Party all last night, why?" "No reason, here's your money." I love that the staff lives to satisfy your every whim. "Can you dye this jacket safety orange and attach jingle bells?" "Yes!" Such attention with respect. Such service without judgment. I get more out of Nordstrom than I ever got out of dating.

Robinsons-May. The Men's Store could be better, but I like that they've separated it from the main store—you know, where all the wives are shopping with their poor husbands whom they've dragged along. "Hold my purse, honey, while I try this on." If I want to see straight men with purses, I'll rent *Braveheart*. That leaves the Men's Store mainly to gay men and to women shopping for their husbands because most straight men don't know how to shop for clothes. (If you think I'm overgeneralizing, think back. Last time you saw your dad, what was he wearing?) Now the complaint I have with the Men's Store Robinsons-May is the help have a li-i-ittle attitude. Some of us are always going to have love handles. Some of us have not made peace with that. I would be one of those people. So I get a tad testy when some West Hollywood 24-Hour Fitness twinkie smirks when as I ask if Guess? makes 36-29 jeans, then says, "No, sir. Not that we would carry. Perhaps you should try Millers Outpost." Oh, yeah? Perhaps you should just bite me. Sometimes you just have to say, "Excuse me, I shop here, you work here."

Another store that bothers me is Banana Republic. What happened? In the '80s this store prided itself on carrying nothing but terrific safari wear. Even ordering from the catalog was an adventure—no pictures, just an artist's rendering. But the descriptions! "A classic cut makes these pants perfect for going directly from six hours in your two-seater biplane to a photo op with the ambassador waiting for you at Giza. Khaki cotton pant, $29." Just say that out loud: Khaki cotton pant, khaki cotton pant. Dontcha just wanna say "cha-cha-cha" after it? And that's what I miss. They were selling romance, dreams of treks across the Gobi, Amazonian discovery. I'll never ride the road to Mandalay, but damn it, I could look the part. "Marge, see that man? He just got back from Cairo!" "How can you tell?" "He's wearing the khaki cotton pant, cha-cha-cha." But they don't have a catalog any more. Gone are the go-anywhere, do-anything cottons that last forever. Now they sell suits of silk. Dry-clean-only polyesters. Aromatherapy candles, fer cryin' out loud. Their pants start at $98, they're made of rayon, and they're out of style by the time you get them altered. I quit going to Banana Republic when they started selling cashmere. Rest in peace, old Banana Republic, I remember you fondly.

But there's still Bloomingdale's. Where the men all look so shiny and new, I swear they come shrink-wrapped. Every one shaved, powdered, plucked, tweezed, and FDS'ed into a stupor. And the hair! There's more mousse in Bloomingdale's than in all of Canada. And they know flattery will get you to buy anything. You will not find men so willing to tell you what you want to hear without dialing 976 first. And it's almost as cheap. So I'm told. I was holding up a T-shirt in a cunning shade of teal when a salesman approached. He was gorgeous and tanned and blond and about as old as my car. He looked at me with the most earnest blue eyes and said, "That looks fabulous on you, you're gonna want at least ten." Yes, he was outrageously presumptuous, but isn't it cute? Anyway, I declined, and he asked if I'd seen the other neon colors. I said no, where are they? He touched my arm and said, "I'll show you." He touched my arm. I tried to imagine my father if a salesman ever touched him. I wondered if it would be my father who would leave the store first or the salesman flying backwards. I followed my salesman, loved the neon colors, and bought nine more. So much for curbing my shopping habit. Bloomingdale's, you've got me where I live.

PUTTING IT ALL TOGETHER AT IKEA

I have a love-hate relationship with Ikea. I love the lure of inexpensive knockdown furniture. I hate having to take three days of provisions with me because I know it will take that long to find my way out. I suspect "Ikea" is Swedish for "rat maze"—make that "really, really *big* rat maze" because the smallest Ikea going is still the size of Delaware. But you have to love a store that used a gay couple in its advertising, and, of course, can satisfy a craving for lingonberries.

Not long ago Fred and I needed a chest of drawers. We took a deep breath and entered Ikea. Near the entrance is the children's recreation area, a room full of plastic balls. It was filled with adults. I think these people were left there as toddlers and matured while waiting for their parents to emerge with affordable window treatments. Fred felt it was an ominous sign.

We started our trek through living rooms, dining rooms, easy chairs, wall units, coffee tables, sofas, wall units, coffee tables, sofas, wall units, coffee tables... Oh, hell. We were stuck in a dreaded Ikea loop. This is what happens to people just prior to appearing on milk cartons. I suspect Amelia Earhart will be discovered one day wandering between Peg-Board shelving and kitchens. We were lucky to find an experienced bwana, who helped us hack our way through dinette sets and bedrooms to arrive at chests of drawers.

Once there we had to decide which unpronounceable Ikea style we wanted. Fred liked the Glemphengoople, but I leaned toward the more austere Blarf. We compromised on an eight-drawer cherry veneer Fartengrump. We already had Poontzen bedside tables from an earlier foray, and we felt the Fartengrump would complement our Poontzens. At least they would speak the same language.

A native took our order and gave us a computer printout we were to take to the cashier at the exit. A short week later we found the exit and forked over $350—a steal. Then we took the computer printout to a department that actually fetched the box of ingeniously designed plastic and pressed wood chips that would become our cherry Fartengrump. I was so relieved! I was afraid we'd have to go in the warehouse to get it ourselves, and we were running low on food and water.

We got The Box and loaded it into my little VW Fox. It stuck dangerously far out the window and Fred had to lie on the floor in the back for the ride home, but we were so excited to see blue sky again, we didn't care. Plus all the signs were in English.

Once home, Fred started dinner while I opened The Box. All the pieces were there, of course. One thing Ikea is very good at is making sure you are supplied with everything you need to be completely bewildered. Our Fartengrump would be held together by some odd nail-screw-pin combination. At right angles to these would go even more bizarre-looking round screw-clamp jobbies. God knows what the Swedish words for these things are, no doubt countless syllables long, filled with dozens of umlauts and "ø"s. Too much to ponder. I decided to call them Bobs and Joes. It felt empowering to give same-sex English names to foreign doodads, plus I wouldn't be merely building furniture, I'd be matchmaking. Now, to work!

Ikea doesn't give you written instructions on how to put your stuff together. They give you pictures. The set of directions I was up against had precise orthographic projections showing that the Bobs and Joes were to be inserted, but not into the sides the drawing presented. Rather, there were detailed arrows showing that a Joe was supposed to clamp onto a Bob *around the corner* from what the drawing gave me. Perhaps the Swedes feel whatever these metal pieces do should be done in private. That or there's an instruction designer named Sven laughing up his lederhosen or whatever it is that vindictive Swedes wear. Whichever, the end result is frustration and a reason to start hating Volvos.

After an hour I managed to decipher how Bob fit on a peg with Joe holding him securely in place. I was chagrined it took me so long to figure it out when half the porno I own shows just such an arrangement. Nevertheless, I felt I had cracked the Enigma Code. Still, that was only drawing number 1. There were seven more to go. I am painfully aware I am not the world's smartest man, but Stephen Hawking couldn't understand this. Fred offered to help. "No!," I shouted. "This is *my* life journey! Get away!"

I spent forever staring at these cryptic drawings. Hieroglyphics were child's play next to this, but I was making progress. If I could figure out these, I could decipher anything—the mysteries of the pyramids, Aztec calendars, crop circles, alternate side of the street parking. The Joe grips the Bob that fits in the slat that holds the drawer that connects to the frame... Hey, I was beginning to get this! And lo, ere a fortnight had passed, I had a fully functional Fartengrump!

I never felt so masculine in my life! True, there were an awful lot of leftover Bobs, Joes, and pegs, but testosterone surged through me, allowing me to deem them "unnecessary." I felt invincible. Hell, I could put the Parthenon back together armed with only an Allen wrench and a misleading diagram—*and* do it at below department store prices! Today I am a man.

PUTTING PARKING IN ITS PLACE

There is a parking god in Los Angeles who must be served. This unholy demon demands payment from newcomers, who are hit with flurries of parking tickets upon arrival—the initial sacrifice for having the temerity to trespass within these city limits. Those of us who have lived here for years also must offer up periodic payments on an irregular basis at this foul god's pleasure and whim. You can go months without a ticket, then one day you park, dash to your friend's house to drop off those Colt videos you "borrowed" while house-sitting, return to your car *30 seconds later,* and you have been ticketed. You see no parking troll walking away, nor vehicle leaving. It appears a ticket has spontaneously generated under your windshield wiper. This is the work of the Devil.

In case you couldn't guess, I got a parking ticket today. I was unable to properly translate the myriad signs invoking vehicular vengeance for parking between the hours of naught and noon on alternate Tuesdays unless there is also occurring a neap tide or gibbous moon.

What kind of a person would take such a parasitic position as parking demon anyway? What black-hearted hellkite grows up dreaming of visiting misery on automobile owners? Clearly, they are a cunning and diabolical lot. One time I parked by a grassy area where there were no meters. I noticed holes in the ground but thought nothing of them. I returned to find the holes filled with concrete supporting shiny new meters and that my car had been ticketed.

These people are vultures—no, lower than vultures because vultures don't have quotas. And don't tell me they're just doing their job. I know what kind of job they do. This morning I parked on a nearly empty street with clearly posted two-hour parking. I went inside for a 45-minute Weight Watchers meeting and returned to find that every car on my side of the street had been ticketed, including cars that hadn't even been there when I parked. Down the street coming my way was a parking enforcement vehicle with two parking fascists inside, methodically writing tickets for each car on the street. One man drove while the other wrote the tickets and shoved them under the wiper, so arrogant, smug, and hound-dog lazy they didn't even bother getting out of the car to do it.

My eyes narrowed with ugly purpose, the delicious black bloom of outrage spread through my soul. I was the arm of God sent to smite these jackbooted tyrants, and smite I would, hammer and tongs. My imminent triumph would be in the name of every Weight Watcher who had not yet returned to his car as well as every other ill-used citizen parked on this street and streets like it the world over. Mine was the righteous cause of justice provoked. Besides, I had gained two pounds that week, so I was already plenty pissed off.

I forced them to stop by throwing my above-goal self in front of their slow moving car. "How dare you ticket every car on this street?" I demanded.

"They are all in violation of the two-hour limit," said the driver, smiling infuriatingly in his imperiously profane power.

I coolly explained to them that the other cars had arrived after I had parked there a mere 45 minutes earlier and that they were both going to inhabit the ring of hell Dante reserved for dissembling liars and evil ruthless pricks spawned by whores.

"Look, pal," the driver said, "we have ways of telling how long you parked."

"Name the method you and your Gestapo monkey-boy used!" I challenged the driver loudly. "I defy thee!" When I truly lose it I become not only apoplectic but apocalyptic. I speak like the King James Version of the Bible, and it has an effect. Unfortunately it is not the one I would choose. Rather than gazing in awe and cowering at my terrible countenance, people gawk as if I were Howard Beale in the movie *Network* on his second day without medication. It also doesn't help that my terrible countenance gets all puckered and red like a baboon's backside. By the time this happens, though, I am unable to stop myself. "Show unto me your methods!"

"We put chalk on the tires."

"Aha!" I screamed several octaves too high for any dramatic purpose whatsoever. "I see no chalk! None! No chalk on yon tires!"

"Or sometimes we put a penny behind the tire to tell if a car has moved."

"Show me the penny!" I shouted Cuba Gooding Jr.–like, pounding on the hood, "*Show me the penny*!" About this time I was thinking I really should have had breakfast before weighing in, but I forced that thought back because I knew I had them red-handed. "You cannot show me pennies because thar be none!" I was shifting from Middle English to Early Pirate. Not a good sign.

"Listen," the incubus with sulfur breath hissed, "I'm gonna write you up for interfering in our duty if you don't let us proceed."

"Ha ha ha ha!" I cackled in salty triumph, planting both hands firmly on the hood of their car. "With me standing here in front of ye? Ye can't proceed! Ye'll have to run me down first!"

Foul Beelzebub turned to Baal and raised an eyebrow. He threw the car in reverse and hit the gas. With jaw agape, I could only watch them recede down, down, down the block. I slumped as the car dwindled in size until it stopped and turned down the alleyway, headed, no doubt, for another street to continue making their quotas in quotidian fashion. I was alone in the middle of the street. Time stood still. A dog barked in the distance.

With one final spasm of bitter choler and gall I did a writhing dance of rage and impotence, cursing heaven passionately. I swore, spittle flying, with such venom and wrath it brought citizens to their windows and balconies. Most applauded. I was so livid that I actually punched my car. My hand is fine, but the dent will be another $200.

So once again the parking god has been fed. And once again it was not the parking laws but the person who has been violated. And once again I have a feeling my therapist will be very busy with me next Tuesday at 4 o'clock.

FUNNY IS WHERE YOU FIND IT

I was having lunch with a friend last week when, out of the blue, he asked where I was getting such funny ideas. I said, "I'm sorry, I thought I was kicking the table." Still, it made me wonder where I find humor. For me, the answer is: pretty much everywhere.

Take shopping—always a great place to start for anything. Believe it or not, I found a place in southern California gayer than the West Hollywood International Male store. It's Restoration Hardware. I go to the one in Century City Shopping Center, and it's so filled with fabulous froufrou and cunning objets d'art that even straight men who wander in start clutching pearls. You can actually hear their hypothalamuses shrink as they fall under the spell of egg-and-dart molding, oversized chenille pillows, and pineapple finials. "Oh, Linda, look at this tasseled velvet runner! Couldn't you just *die*!" Men who are already gay get even gayer. I saw two men walk in with bags from Politix who actually lifted right off the floor. My straight friend Emile says it's just Pottery Barn on steroids, but I beg to differ. Restoration Hardware is to Pottery Barn what Pottery Barn is to Sears. Even Emile was unable to leave without purchasing the queerest candle sconces you've ever seen. Straight men purchasing sconces is one of the biblical signs of the apocalypse. Oh, well, at least when it happens he'll be nicely lit.

I thought it was humorous when Fred and I had to shop for a new place to live a couple of years ago. We wanted to keep the money in the community, so we turned to *Frontiers* magazine. You may have heard of it. *Frontiers* is a gay rag that sometimes buys stuff I write so I can afford, oh, gas. My second-favorite part of the magazine is the classifieds, through which we found our lovely new home, although it took some doing.

The interior of the first place we looked at, including ceiling, fixtures, and floor, was painted entirely in black. We passed on that one because we had two black cats and knew we'd never be able to find them. Another place was in a small complex where we were not allowed to see the actual apartment. Instead, we were assured by the manager: "Honest, is like mine just, you like?" His had a goat. We decided to pass on our chance at in-house feta and continued our quest. Fred had circled a listing in the gay ghetto, so we checked that one out next. It was a gay-owned building with a gay manager, and when we arrived the all-gay tenants in their gay designer swimwear were lounging gaily by the gay pool. Festive? It was like falling into a Fire Island mai tai. We just didn't have the energy for it, so we left. One of my straight friends, who's a stand-up comedian, couldn't understand why we didn't move in immediately. I asked him to imagine living in a 48-unit complex of nothing but stand-up comedians. He said, "Oh."

Speaking of places populated by homosexuals, Bloomingdale's liked a piece I wrote recently. It was on the joys of shopping at their fine store, and they loved what I said so much, they sent me a goodie bag full of stuff. I was so angry. *Why* hadn't I written about shopping at *Tiffany's*?

Fred thinks it's humorous that I see gay men everywhere; they don't even have to be real. For instance, at the grocery I see the Brawny Paper Towel man as gay, which is hardly a stretch. No straight man would ever be that well-groomed in the woods because he wouldn't have thought to bring his Clinique cream shave, postshave healer, and José Eber mousse. The Jolly Green Giant may be green, but he's buffed. Plus—ho, ho, ho!—he appeals to the size queen in me. And have you ever seen a female Keebler elf? In my mind those elves are up to plenty more in that hollow tree besides cookies. "Hey, fellas, who wants to lick my beaters?"

I see humor in myself when I'm at church. It's a primarily gay congregation with a goodly share of lookers. Come time to greet each other in the spirit of love, I have to be careful who and how I hug, or I'll end up having to hold a hymnal in front of me.

My therapist has helped me to see the humor in my childhood. I was a fat little boy. After supper I'd join my family in their dessert: a single petite scoop of Winn-Dixie Superbrand ice milk. Then, later, I'd sneak out back and shotgun a can of pie filling. Whenever my family would leave me alone in the house I would happily watch TV while eating mayonnaise right from the jar, chased by spoonfuls of Swiss Miss dry. I loved holidays because eating was encouraged and I could even eat in public. No more shamefully hiding cornbread stuffing under my bed next to the *Playgirl* magazines. Oh, what a painful line of thought this has become. I take it back; nothing about my childhood was funny. Remind me to get a new therapist.

Sometimes friends will tell me a wonderfully dark story and all I have to do is pass it along—like the one about a certain handsome well-known local ad executive we'll call Bob, who wanted to go to a bathhouse but was afraid. After a particularly rotten day at work, he decided to hell with it, he was going. Once there, he ventured a full two steps out of his room before literally bumping into a client he'd met with that afternoon—who started pitching him an altogether different service than the one he'd offered earlier in the day. Mortified, Bob dashed back to his room, threw his clothes on, and fled. "I am too well known," he told my friend, "I can't risk it in this town." Several months later he was in a different city and

decided to give it another go, figuring after his first experience, how much worse could it get? He entered the steam
room. An elderly man came in and sat next to him. Suddenly,
the older man was pawing at our young executive, making
disturbing, frantic noises. Bob tore out of the steam room and
ran to the lounge, where he sat shaking for 20 minutes until
he could calm down enough to leave. He went up to his room
to get his things and there, in front of his door, was the elderly gentleman—facedown on the floor. An emergency med-
ical team came barreling down the hall lead by the bathhouse
manager, forcefully knocking Bob against the wall. The EMT
men quickly pulled out the electric paddles. "Clear!"
Whamp! Nothing. "Clear!" Whamp! Again, nothing.
Traumatized, his voice quivering, Bob asked if he could please
just get into his room. "No, you heartless shit," bellowed the
manager. "Can't you see this bastard's dead? And show a little respect, asshole, pick up your towel." Thus ended two
men's bathhouse careers.

I find that humor is all around. I see it in an evening with
friends, an encounter in a store, a look in the mirror. It's in my
home, my job, and heaven knows, my bank account. Humor
is out there waiting for you to see it too. My seventh-grade
English teacher, Miss Ballsly, said, "All you need is good spirits and to be able to look at things a little differently." Or, as I
like to put it, a gay heart and a queer point of view.

ILL-SERVICED

A couple of weeks ago I had that bug that's been going around. This was not good, because when I am sick I regress to the emotional age of 2. I want people to bring me any and everything I ask for and I want it brought now, *Now*, NOW! If there is a problem or any delay whatsoever, I can't cope. You have not seen ugly until I start moaning in obnoxiously high decibels and a bathrobe. At home Fred knows to put everything I might possibly need on the bedstand and flee the house until I become human again. Going out in public is an especially bad idea. Unfortunately, I was out of cold medicine and desperate for something that would give relief.

Driving in a sick stupor (OK, a Dodge Neon, same thing), I straddled the double yellow line that I knew led down the street to the drugstore. I parked across several handicapped spaces and staggered into the ghastly glare of far too many fluorescents. These hideous lights make *healthy* people look like trauma victims. Stumbling past a display of mirrors, I saw that I looked like an extra on *Buffy*. "Oh, God," I groaned irritably, loudly, "where is the medici-i-ine!"

Don't these idiots know they should have the one item I want right by the entrance? In fact, how dare they sell anything else? These stores sell too much other crap anyway. I bumped into lawn chairs and a display of Alpo. When did we start demanding that our pharmacy carry deck furniture and dog food? What store manager dreamed of a place where you could pick up Xanax, Moon Pies, an enema, and wine in a box? It should be a felony for a pharmacy to sell anything but medicine, damn it, and there I was staring at cans of Turtle Wax. I had a fever, I was dizzy, nauseous, and by now furious that I couldn't find pharmaceuticals in a phreaking pharmacy. One of the rare employees tried to skulk by at the end of the aisle. "You!" I shouted, lurching after him like Robert Downey Jr. at the end of his methadone, "Cure me!" I caught him trying to escape down an aisle of party streamers and flip-flops. I grabbed him by his uniform shirt and whipped him around so I could breathe hot contagion at him, growling, "This is a drugstore. Where the fuck are your *drugs*?"

Evidently they are used to this sort of thing. He calmly led me two aisles over—past bath salts and bakeware—to the cold medicines. Then the bastard disappeared.

Comtrex, Dimetapp, Vicks, Robitussin, how am I supposed to choose from all these? I'm sick, for crying out loud, don't ask me to think. Every brand has seven different formulas, each covering a different permutation of a lengthy list of symptoms. This one's for cough, sore throat, headache, and body aches, but that one's for cough, runny nose, sore throat, and has an expectorant but nothing for body aches. OK, try to think: I have congestion, nausea, can't sleep, a fever, dry skin, brittle hair, a loose filling, and body odor.

Then my tiny addled brain saw the solution: Drugstores should have someone stationed right at the front, an older lady with a sweet, friendly, maternal face. As soon as you stagger in she'll recognize you are sick, come forward, and take your hand. "Oh, my poor baby," she'll say, "tell me what's wrong." She'll pull your head to her breast, which smells soothingly of mothballs, pumpkin pie, and dusty potpourri, nod sympathetically, and say, "Oh, sweetie, I know just the thing." Then she'll pluck the perfect bottle of medicine for your symptoms. Plus she'll let you pay *her* for it because "You're sick, honey, and shouldn't have to stand in that awful line at the front."

I saw instantly that this policy should be instituted in all stores, not just pharmacies. When I wander into the grocery with that ten-people-for-dinner-tonight-and-I-only-have-20-bucks look on my face, a Graham Kerr type will rush to my side. "Not a problem," he'll say, "all you need is pasta with a garlic cream sauce, a little salad, and bread sticks—all for $19.38." "But what about the wine?" I'll ask. "Simple. Announce that it's your 30-day anniversary. It'll not only shut them up, but they'll be forced to applaud you."

At Bloomingdale's I envision a man who looks like my perfectly groomed bachelor uncle, Bruce, who toured as Rolf in the original *Sound of Music*. He'll say he's been sent by the management to tell me the sales clerk who selected this shirt to go with these pants is not my friend. "But don't be too harsh on him," Uncle Bruce will say. "He has a family to support, and if we don't help straight people raise their children, where will the future homos come from?" He'll then help me find the perfect shirt, whispering confidentially, "Come back and get it next week *when it's on sale*."

I began to further explore my service-friendly fantasy mall. At Williams-Sonoma I'll be met by a young gay man in an apron who looks like an ex–flight attendant, if that's not redundant. "If you're going to get the ten-inch German springform cake pan," he'll insist, "you simply must get the cake decoration stencils too. Presentation, honey, presentation."

Outside of Brookstone I'll find an earth-mother lesbian who won't even let me enter. "No!" she'll shout. "There is absolutely nothing in this store that anyone truly needs!" "But I really, really want that vibrating hammock," I hear myself whining. "It self-warms!" "I'm sorry," she'll say, "but if you have too much money you should take it elsewhere and do something more constructive with it. Like buy crack."

In a macho menswear store Eddie Bauer himself will appear, a big butch urban lumberjack dispatched to help me try on intimate apparel. "Oh, Eddie," I'll call, sticking my head out of the dressing room, "could you come in here and help me out? I don't think it's, um, hanging right."

When I was better a couple of days later, I saw I had been taking medicine for, among other things, diarrhea, asthma, gas, and menstrual cramps, none of which I had. At least not that week. This underscored the need for the elderly matron I had envisioned in the analgesic aisle.

Now that I'm well I say it's time to take the concept of meeting the needs of the customer to a higher level. The next time I go into Rite-Aid I want to be treated like a Japanese pop star in Neiman Marcus. And when I'm in Neiman's, at their prices, the service should finish with a rinse-and-spit. For them, not me. Unless the help is totally hot. Heck, why do you think they call it getting serviced?

CATALOGING MY TIME

I love to shop, but sometimes a body just has to take time out to go to the bathroom. Fortunately, this doesn't stop me because I get catalogs from all over and keep them near the toilet. Given what so many of them are selling it's the only appropriate place. Catalogs are perfect throne room reading because there's no plot to worry about, no thought demanded, and lots of bright colorful pictures. It's fun to imagine who came up with this stuff. More frightening, though, is who would buy it.

For instance, the Fingerhut catalog is a white heterosexual cry for help. On page 9 of the new one they offer sheets, a bedspread, pillow cases, and shams, all depicting the famous painting *End of the Trail* wherein a lone, spent, Native American on horseback realizes there is no stopping the genocide of his people at the hands of whites who will extinguish his culture so they can offer deals on dust ruffles and 50% cotton throws depicting his agony. There's also an *End of the Trail* painting and shield but any description that begins "Hand-painted in oils on velvet" is not worth finishing.

Fingerhut also has bath coordinates so frilly, lacy, beribboned, swagged, and trimmed, it would send Mary Englebreit into a diabetic coma. Does any bathroom truly need a tub skirt? When I saw this I was convinced Fingerhut had an angry and bitter gay designer working there wreaking cruel revenge on straight America, but after seeing the *End of the Trail* stuff I knew it couldn't be true. Any gay would empathize with an antagonized minority facing the strength of an entire nation and forbear.

On page 63 is a picture of Fingerhut food grinders in action. One is squirting a long tube of mealy looking brownish sausage onto a plate where it is landing in a coiled pile. It is disturbingly suggestive of what *I* am doing while flipping through the catalog with the bathroom fan on. It is astonishing to realize there is no trace of intended irony or humor anywhere in the catalog. Fingerhut is a national treasure of unintentional kitsch. It is straight people run amok.

Sometimes it is gays who are completely out of control. I just received a catalog called Gene Book selling expensive 15½-inch tall female dolls named Gene dressed in 1940s and '50s fashions. Gene is the cunning creation of Mel Odom, who is pictured in an inset on the back looking like George Michael's slightly more butch brother. Among Mel's myriad costumes for Gene are "Poolside," "Usherette," "USO Entertainer," "Embassy Luncheon," and "Bridge Club." There's a kicky little number dubbed "Hello, Hollywood, Hello!" dripping in faux fur and glamour. The "Red Venus" ensemble looks like a Tastee-Freez blood clot in taffeta. My favorite is an utterly over-the-top antebellum outfit featuring a lavish bodice of white organza embellished with impossibly tiny white satin braiding and crocheted roses with leaves that, according to the ad copy, caused doll designer Katie McHale to gush, "Designing the 'Savannah' costume for the Gene doll transformed my life!" Something must be done to get Katie out of the house more and to stop this Mel Odom. Sad gay men and straight women with no lives are far too vulnerable to this overwrought piffle.

The Art & Artifact catalog brims with ersatz medieval, gothic, deco, nouveau, you-name-it crap, and it's loads of fun. You can "bring the rare genius of Frank Lloyd Wright onto your table with our stunning coasters." You may be asking yourself when was the last time you were stunned by a coaster. Well, at $53 for a set of four, they certainly stunned me. At least there's an educational benefit to this catalog. Who knew Frank worked in miraculously absorbent soapstone?

This catalog also offers a Monopoly rip-off called Bibleopoly. I have visions of buying up all of Bethlehem, erecting a hotel, and having no room at the inn. I imagine landing on Community Ark and drawing a card that reads "Love Jonathan with a love surpassing that of women; go directly to jail."

Also in the realm of the uplifting-for-profit, Avon offers a mini-catalog called Inspirational Treasures filled with things like Gardening Angels Keepsake Stationery sets and Noah's Ark Inspirational throws. They offer a Jingle Magnet Angel, which is a chubby cherub of unsullied Aryan descent with a single bell dangling from each of her six chakras. Perhaps it's for use in conjunction with one of their other items, a book titled *Devotions for Dieters*. You open your refrigerator and she jingles, reminding you you're fat, and rather than polish off that can of pink frosting, you decide to consult *Devotions for Dieters* to see what God has to say about your flab. Oh, please. I've been on enough diets to know that no Bible verse is gonna stop me from stuffing my face. Hell, it was misrepresented Bible verses that made me feel so lousy about myself that I wanted to pig out in the first place. If Avon really wanted to help dieters, they'd ditch the book and develop zero-calorie Oreos.

Like so many other places, Avon also offers the WWJD bracelet, which stands for "What would Jesus do?" I imagine Avon hoping Jesus would do something like pick up the phone and say, "Hello, Avon? I'd like to order 12 bottles of Skin So Soft. No, wait, make that 11."

I have no idea how I got on the list to receive Atlanta Cutlery, a catalog devoted to knives, swords, battle-axes, throwing stars, and other malicious metal mayhem. On page 30 are Competition Tomahawks. I don't watch ESPN, but are there really contests with these things? How do you win, get the most scalps? They also have genuine Military Issue Kukri Knives from India, the perfect gift, I suppose, for that Gurkha in your life. On the same page is the Parang Nabur, which turns out to be a Malaysian jungle machete and not, as it sounded to me, a Klingon gay bar. Other knives are so fiendishly designed for gory flesh-ripping that you pray the inventor doesn't live in your neighborhood, even though you know he probably does. I will not be ordering from Atlanta Cutlery. Unless, of course the Pat Robertsons drop by for hors d'oeuvres. I wouldn't actually use the knives on them, I'd just set them out with the cheese to give them the willies. "Pat, I think I'd like carving you...some Jarlsberg." I love festive occasions filled with dread.

Which is a perfect segue into marriage. Every couple of years I buy a wedding present from Tiffany's, which is enough for them to send me the catalog regularly. I love Tiffany's because you can get a couple of champagne flutes for 45 bucks. They come in that huge signature blue box with the white bow, which, sitting among wedding gifts from Crate & Barrel, stands out with such a promise of lush opulence as to make the bride and her mother unable to concentrate on the ceremony.

The items in their catalog range from the exquisite to the shockingly crass. I am happy to share a world where there exists an Etoile bracelet in 18k gold with diamonds set in platinum for $3,950 knowing I'll never own it. It is galling, however, to realize there are people with piles of pelf to squander on putrid puffy hearts of solid gold with a gaudy TIFFANY & CO. emblazoned across them just in case anyone missed the point. God creates poor people with taste and rich people with none. It's how we know God has a sense of humor.

Once a year I go to Neiman Marcus and use a credit card to buy a jar of nuts—just so they'll send me their catalog. The Neiman's catalog is second only to International Male in sensuality. I don't know how they do it, but they can make a pair of champagne Prada pumps so sexy that I don't want to wear them, I want to fuck them. Somebody get me the name of that photographer. If he can make handbags look hot, there's hope for me.

The Expressions catalog is named for what I would have on my horrified face if someone ever sent me anything out of it. A $495 hand-painted porcelain birdbath blights the cover of this cloyfest, and it never gets better. According to their own copy, "Swirling rosebuds, dragonflies, foliage, and the ebullient exclamation YOU ARE MY SUNSHINE" cover this waste of clay and glaze, setting the tone for the rest of this catalog. Expressions is crammed full of nasty faux everything, any item of which in a room would drive me from it. On page 52 they have a 17-inch-tall Collector's Musical Tree under glass for $399 that is "handmade in Florida with chenille stems, over 300 ornaments, 35 lights, and hand-wrapped gifts." It plays "We Wish You a Merry Christmas," has a mini-train that chugs back and forth, and, as if such a thing were really necessary, comes with a certificate of authenticity. I can just imagine such a document: "This certificate authenticates that you have purchased the most appalling and glaring example of Yuletide putrescence ever to blot the season. It is a twinkling, cunning horror on so many hideous levels that one cannot look away, try as one might. This obscenity is sure to bring screaming nightmares to children, adults, and pets. It is the singularly most excruciatingly excrementicious piece of tinseled tripe ever to come through the mail. It is certifiably vulgar, toweringly ugly, and a carbuncle on the concept of Christmas. Enjoy it with our good wishes you troglodytic, philistine pig." If that rant seems harsh, remember that it's coming from a Christmas queen who paints gold tips on his poinsettias. But even I have limits.

I love looking through my catalogs, though, whether they be displays of outrageous opulence, grotesquely garish wealth or lurid lack of taste. It's low brain-power entertainment, which is why I keep them stacked on my toilet tank for easy perusal when nature calls. Besides, there's nothing like being able to window-shop with your pants around your ankles.

PART FOUR
Politics and God

POLITICS "LITE"—Activism Made Easy

There's good news! You don't have to become political. You already are. Now, I don't mean to upset you, but if you're reading this, there's a good chance you're gay. That makes you a political hot potato, my dear, and as far as most of the country is concerned, about as welcome as a kreplach at a Klan rally. The very fact that gays exist upsets a lot of people, most of whom I couldn't be happier upsetting. But bigots are out there and up to high mischief. You know, little things like denying you rights, jobs, children, medicine, and the ability to carry this flaming homo book to your car without wondering if you're going to be attacked for it. Your choice is to go into hiding, whereby you hand them political victory, or become politically butch, stand up with your big limp wrists on your nelly little waist, and say "I don't *think* so!"

I know, I know, you don't care about politics. Since the Democrats turned into Republicans it's hard to get excited about anything in Washington outside of Dupont Circle. But what are ya gonna do? These folks want us dead, the kookies, and they are organized something fierce. So right off the bat we're in trouble. No one I know can organize anything more complicated than a sit-down dinner for ten. I notice, however, that every month in the gay community there's at least one wild party with multiple DJs, a live show, and an exotic sex-charged theme that somehow manages to come off without a hitch. That tells me we *can* organize, we just need to figure a way to make politics sexy. We need a Town Hall

Meeting with community leaders, DJs, and lube. We need a Gay Rights Rally and Sling Party. Somebody get the National Gay and Lesbian Task Force, Tom of Finland, and Chi Chi LaRue, and let's get this show on the road.

If political functions aren't your scene, that's OK. You're plenty political right where you are—as long as you are what you are. Simply being visible is one of the best things you can do. Are you out at work, or are you wasting energy "passing"? If you're a male and you've ever admitted you liked *The Bridges of Madison County*, organized the Secret Santa, or taken the day off for the Academy Awards, trust me, darling, you're not fooling anyone. If you're a woman and you've ever brought in pictures of your cats or your vacation just happens to coincide with the Dinah Shore classic every year, you might as well wear a sign. So stop using the wrong pronoun when talking about your lover and give those straight folks something better to talk about other than Pop Warner Football. Put a rainbow sticker on your car and let everybody know what it means. This is a political gesture that will also make you a better driver. As a representative of the entire gay community you'll think twice before cutting off family vans and station wagons.

Furthermore, letting people know you're gay gives you enormous power you can use anywhere. Next time you hear another tired "don't drop the soap" joke, stand up and tell that person they are not funny; they're cliché. Next time you're at a straight wedding and they play "YMCA" at the reception, tell the groom's parents exactly what the song their son is dancing to so enthusiastically is really about. Next time some moron calls you a lousy queer, take offense and tell them, on the contrary, you're a *fantastic* queer. Be out, be seen.

So what does being out do for you politically? It enlightens and changes fundamental thinking. I have several straight friends who have told me I was the first homosexual they had ever known. They now know that I, a homo, am not the monster they'd been told to expect, unless of course they call and wake me early Sunday after the White Party. Talk about politics lite, I didn't even realize I was effecting change. I feel like the woman in the commercial curled up on her sofa sipping coffee saying "I'm cleaning my oven!" Picture me on a chenille throw with a cup of Stonewall Brew, "I'm eradicating hate!" The great thing is, the effect of my being out is permanent because once a person learns something, they can't unlearn it. When my straight friends hear "gay" they think of my smiling furry face, not the slathering, evil, lust-filled portrait Mr. Falwell tries to paint. I mix with my friends' families, educating more minds, and they no longer worry I'm going to emit gay rays and make their kids turn out queer. (Although I do have a suspicion about little Eric; in seven or eight years I may have to be a role model. Ugh, the pressure!)

If you're part of a long term committed couple, married, as it were, you're political as all get-out. You're confounding the religious right as well as gay party boys. Fred and I love doing that. On one side, we're a threat to millions of heterosexuals with failed relationships, and on the other, we've got bitchy queens thinking, *Why would two gays want to emulate a straight stereotype?* I don't know about other couples, but we do it so we can swap clothes. Actually, we aren't officially married. After 19 years, what's the point? We already have dinnerware we don't use. Politically, though, it would be nice to have the same rights as hetero couples. Far from destroying the institution of marriage (and what is the religious right scared of, having to select tasteful wedding gifts?), I think we'd be a breath of fresh air.

Fred and I recently received an announcement from a gay couple preparing for a holy union. They're registered at Neiman Marcus, Home Depot, and the Pleasure Chest, our local sex toy and fetish store. Can you imagine such a statement of glamour, practicality, and eroticism from your cousin

Ira's wedding to Cindy Lou? Because of the politically charged nature of gay marriage, Fred and I have decided we'll go ahead and get married—just as soon as we figure out how we can register at the Money Store.

Your every choice and action is political simply because you are gay. There's nothing you can do about it except use it. I can even make it easy for you: Go to Disneyland, watch *Will & Grace,* buy another pair of Levi's. Suddenly activism feels like shopping, so what's not to like?

OK, I know you don't want to be political. I didn't either, but I'll tell you what my friend told me years ago when I was whining to him, "You wouldn't be saying this if you knew how nonpolitical I really was." His reply?

"But ya *are,* Blanche. Ya *are.*"

GAY ACTIVISM—The Straight Dopes

Until recently, I thought consciousness was what you hoped to retain after too many hits of poppers. The closest I got to gay activism was boycotting one bottle of Coors in favor of two bottles of Bud. I wasn't developing consciousness, just a beer gut. The word *activism* itself was a turnoff. It sounded too, well, active. My idea of activity is rooting through the sofa cushions for the remote. Using that remote, though, as well as the occasional magazine, I've discovered some amazing things our enemies are saying about us, things that would be hysterical if they weren't so misdirected and the consequences so dire.

For instance, California state senator Pete Knight says, "They're luring kids into homosexual behavior." Ya know, he's right. I remember how it happened to me. A man dressed far too well for Wilmington, N.C., came to my junior high school and lured me with a speech I remember to this day: "C'mon, little Joel, being a fat, acne-covered teenager isn't bad enough. Being terrorized by bullies on a generic basis isn't making your existence the perfect misery it could be. My boy, you need to become a homosexual." It sounded too good to be true. I wanted to know more, and where he got his shoes. "Barneys New York." he said. "Now try to concentrate. How would you like a sporty new nickname?" "Better than Lard-Ass?" I asked. "Much better," he smiled, "How about Homo, Fag, Queer, or even Cocksucker? Think of the character you'll develop from the constant taunting and beatings. Does all this sound like fun or what?" He frowned, seeing I was wavering. "Oh, all right," he said, "I'll throw in the shoes, too. Now whaddaya say?" Well! What could I do when faced with a bargain like that? I volunteered immediately and got the *Liza With a Z* album as an early-signing bonus. Right. I'd love to ask Pete Knight what the hell he's talking about. Does he have a brain cell?

Directly under Pete Knight, as it were, is Pete LaBarbera of Americans for Truth About Homosexuality. LaBarbera, according to the National Affairs report in *Rolling Stone,* "regularly goes undercover to gay rights meetings, gay bars, and other locales, then recounts in near-pornographic detail episodes of fellatio, masturbation, and sadomasochistic sex that he claims to observe." All I can say is, how does he find these places on his own when I can't locate them with a *Damron Guide,* a Ferrari handbook, and the local gay rag? Maybe I should start hanging out with LaBarbera.

Our good friend Fred Phelps was quoted, also in *Rolling Stone,* as saying, "The average fag fellates 106 men, swallows 50 seminal discharges, has 72 penile penetrations of the anus, and ingests feces of 23 different men every year." We wish! Well, maybe not that last part. It's only May, and I am so far behind I'll have to quit my job and spend the rest of the year kneeling, supine, or prone just to catch up with my gay brethren. Here's a news flash, Phelps: We're men; we lie about sex. I wanna know who it is Phelps is talking to that's feeding him this kind of shit. But, in that he ingested it, doesn't that leave him only 22 more to go?

In that same article, a Dr. Paul Cameron says, "If…all you want is the most satisfying orgasm you can get—and that is what homosexuality seems to be—then homosexuality seems too powerful to resist." Dearie me, can you say closet case? "The evidence is that men do a better job on men and women on women," he says, "if all you're are looking for is orgasm." Orgasm, schmorgasm, everyone I know—gay or straight—is looking for stability, a sense of humor, and a willingness to hang around for breakfast. He goes on, "I'm convinced that lesbians are particularly good seducers." They probably are, but I'm guessing it has less to do with lesbian seduction than a certain brand of straight men. "Golly, Marge, you mean if I turn lesbo our lovemaking will last more than five minutes, I won't have to deal with my abusive boyfriend's demeaning patriarchal bullshit, I'll have someone who actually listens when I say something, and all I have to do is put up with your cats? I'm in!" Dr. Cameron is further quoted as saying, "Marital sex tends toward the boring end." Which raises the question, Which end are they boring? But I'm interrupting. "Generally," he says, "it doesn't deliver the kind of sheer sexual pleasure that homosexual sex does." Here is a straight man complaining about straight sex and straight people are listening to him. What is wrong with this picture?

The amazing thing is that this lunacy is typical. Remember the 1996 Defense of Marriage Act? It was rammed through Congress by Bob Barr, a man who believes so strongly in marriage that, after two divorces, he is currently enjoying his third round of marital bliss. Am I the only person getting the joke?

The Christian right regularly predicts that if homosexuality is allowed to run rampant, society will collapse. Don't you think it's more likely that if homosexuality were to run rampant the collective taste of the country would improve and only Wal-Mart and Sears would suffer?

Earlier I asked if Pete Knight had a brain cell. Sadly, he does, and it's a tiny, narrow-minded, hate-filled cell. He votes against basic civil rights for gays despite the fact his own son is gay. Thanks, Dad! He votes against funding for HIV/AIDS prevention and treatment despite the fact his own brother died of AIDS. He's just not an "Up With People" kinda guy. He recently sponsored the Knight initiative that appeared on the California ballot in March of 2000. This measure targeted same-sex couples for discriminatory treatment and was one of the ugliest antigay hatefests since the Holocaust. I really hate the idea of living with laws written by bigoted morons like Knight. It's bad enough I have to pay his salary. I think next year I'll pay my California state tax in cash, in $1 bills with QUEER MONEY stamped on every one in pink. At least then I'll know he won't take any of it.

Knight, Phelps, Barr, Cameron, LaBarbera, and many, many others are indeed grim jokes, but these idiots are out to get you, my pretty, and your little dog too. As long as they can keep their followers wrapped in ignorance they can work their fear tactics against us nationwide. It's up to us to fight back. We need to educate people, starting with our own. If there's anything gays do really well, it's yak on the phone, so pick it up and start using your 5-cent Sundays. Tell people what's happening and what they can do about it. Rule number 1: Vote! It's fun, it takes no time, and where I live you get a smart little I VOTED! sticker to wear and feel superior about all day. Rule number 2: Be out, be seen, and be known to straights. Once their faceless "monster" actually gets a face, and it's as exfoliated and moisturized as yours, it'll be a lot harder to for them to support hate legislation. (Studies prove this!) Think of it, you'll be doing the world a favor just by being yourself! But then, you always knew that, didn't you?

YOU KIDS!

Ah, youth. I walked past the gay bar Rage in West Hollywood the other night, and I don't think I saw anyone inside who was born before the Bicentennial. God love these kids, they're only doing what kids do. Which is to say, each other. At their age I was knotted up in fear and self-loathing, trying to convince my mother I was just keeping those 20 issues of *Playgirl* under my bed for my friend Susie so *her* mother wouldn't find them. (Mom bought it. Remind me to write a piece on my family and denial.) By the time I was 21 I had fooled around furtively with maybe three guys and one girl. In college I had exactly one sexual experience. It was with Monica Bohula. It involved peanut butter and did not go well. Raging with hormones yet constantly frustrated, I bought Vaseline by the drum. My friends and I would get together and commiserate. Years later I found out most of them were doing each other and keeping quiet about it. Some friends.

I look at the freedom and exuberance of today's youth and want to celebrate. You're out, you're open, and with all the trends, you're more entertaining than you could possibly imagine. I see you going to raves in various getups and am vastly satisfied. Why? Because in 20 years you're going to look back at the photos and cringe the same way I do when I see snapshots of me in giant wing collars, striped flares, and pukka shells.

Am I dating myself? My age falls into that vague middle

ground somewhere between chicken and tribal elder. A young man asked me if I identified with younger gays or older gays. I hadn't thought about it. I've been trying, however unsuccessfully, to identify with wealthy gays. It turns out he was talking about the current controversy about "bareback" sex. At first I thought he was saying "bear" back sex, and I'm always up for that. Then I realized the term meant sex without condoms. It's an issue that includes the insane trend of having unprotected sex, often on drugs—no self-esteem issues there, huh?—with lots of partners. Somehow these folks feel they are making a political statement with indiscriminate, unprotected sex, which I don't understand. You do not need sex to make a political statement unless you're buying into the stereotype the religious right is spreading. And what do they know about gays anyway? They think the White Party is headed by David Duke.

This young man felt that older gays were trying to dictate how younger men should have sex. I think he was missing the point. *Surviving* gays are trying to keep others—young, old, and in between—from becoming panels on the Quilt. In case you haven't noticed, we do not reproduce (though goodness knows Fred and I keep trying), so the concept of having fewer of us dying off is desirable. This isn't being prudish. I haven't heard anybody say, "Stop having sex." And if someone did say that, it must have happened when I was in the steam room. Heck, I believe you should be having sex right now. Well, finish this piece first. And then wash your hands.

Until there's an outright cure, indiscriminate unprotected sex is just a form of self abuse—far beyond anything I was doing with Vaseline. And I had an arm like a tennis pro. Besides, do you really want sex with just anybody? There is a difference, my dear, between being a good-time gal and being a slut. All I'm saying is have sex, just stick around so you can keep having it, huh? If nothing else, every queer who manages to stay alive pisses off the Religious Wrong just that much more. Besides, getting older is not such a bad thing.

I'm actually looking forward to getting older. Not to the paunch and the pains and the damn punks at McDonald's calling me "sir," but to the intellectual rewards. As I get older I find I have an increased tolerance for others and a decrease in ambient rage. I still have rage and plenty of it, it's just more focused. If you don't believe me, ask those snot-nosed twinkies at McDonald's. I also have gained a modicum of human understanding and forgiveness. At this rate I figure I will be completely understanding and forgiving about the time I reach 250. That's years, not pounds, and thank you for asking, bitch. Whoops, see what I mean? Got a long way to go. But I'm in it for the long haul because by the time I get up there, gray will be stylish. Let me tell you how I know this.

I'm a back-door baby boomer. That means I was born toward the end of the boom. As boomers aged, we became the consumers who defined the times. That's why Pepsi urged us to "Think Young" in the '60s. It's also why TV is filled with Centrum Silver and Ensure ads now. Yes, you have us to thank for June Allyson in your living room. The cool thing is, now that boomers are old, old is cool. Especially if you own stock in Metamucil. The earlier and therefore older boomers have paved the way, so when I get there I am going to be "all that" and a bag of prunes.

And so are you, my young darlings. You too will get the wrinkles, the arch supports, and, if you're lucky, the wisdom that goes with coming of age. Try not to fear having birthdays. As my 74-year-old father says, they're much better than the alternative.

ROCK-A MY SOUL

Damn, did I hate God. I thought, "Why do I need a God that beats me up every Sunday when I'm already unhealthy enough do that on my own any day of the week?" So I said farewell to religion, and in fact the entire state of North Carolina, going back only to visit at Christmas.

Now, I love to visit my parents, but during every trip there comes a time when I *must* get out of the house or I will do something that makes what Lizzie Borden did look like a bad hair day. The gay bars in Wilmington are good for about ten minutes each, which kills 20 minutes. What, then, to do with the rest of the evening? On one trip I wound up at the Metropolitan Community Church—wondering what the hell in Wilmington could be considered even remotely metropolitan. Sitting there in the comfort of other gays, for the first time I heard the shocking message, which is: God loves you just the way you are. Duh! Funny how some churches lost that somewhere along the way. Long story short: I came back to L.A. and joined Metropolitan Community Church of Los Angeles on Santa Monica Boulevard in West Hollywood.

I don't know what you may have heard about MCCLA. While I was shopping in the ultratrendy Beverly Center once, I actually overheard something like this: "Would you believe it? Gays and lesbians have their own church. I hear they even let those AC-DCs and sex-changed people in. Homosexual, bisexual, transsexual, it sounds so...*sexual*. If God knew what these people were doing, He'd roll over in His grave."

Well, I am happy to say that the reports of God's death are greatly exaggerated. God is very much alive at MCCLA.

I make no claim that MCC is for everybody. Several other denominations are finally getting a clue that a little healing might be nice and forming reconciling congregations. There are gay temples to be found too. But MCCLA is what works for me. Before you come, however, I think there are a few things you should know.

First off, the preacher's a lesbian, which, for folks used to a man standing in the pulpit, can be a problem—something along the lines of "I don't mind a lesbian, I just wish it wasn't a woman." Some men are threatened by a woman in a leadership position. I am threatened by anything high-tech, like a toaster, so I empathize. But I also eat toast. Get over it. Some time ago my brother, who is a Methodist minister in North Carolina, was transferred to a congregation of mainly elderly people who were up in arms that the church had recently sent them a female pastor. When my brother arrived he was met with hosanna praises, and within a month he had buried six members. I've met people from this church, and I know every one of those who died had been waiting until they could get a nonfemale to preach at their funeral. My brother's most important assets were a penis and a shovel.

Man, woman, straight, gay, it's the message that's important, not the messenger. That said, I feel MCCLA is blessed with Nancy Wilson (the preacher, not the singer), a particularly dynamic messenger. She makes me proud. She makes me happy. She also makes me think. I'll forgive her for that, though, because she makes me laugh too. Part of a pastor's job is to rattle people's spiritual cages. They need to be rattled because they are indeed cages from which we need to free ourselves, so I am glad to have this female lesbian pastor. Especially since male lesbians are so hard to come by.

At MCCLA and other MCCs you will encounter inclusive, nonsexist language. For instance, "Our Father" is not in heaven, but "Our Parent" is. "Thy kingdom" will not be coming, but "your realm" will. Hymns I thought I knew have other lyrics. Usually I can anticipate the changes unless it's at the end of the line, then I'm scrambling through the hymnal to see what the new line is and exactly how it's going to rhyme with "mentor." Traditionalists may roll their eyes, but if you've ever been left out, you will appreciate the effort to bring everyone together. Some people claim this is a perversion of God's word, which gives me pause because, after all, these are the people who would know about perverting God's word. Frankly I'm happy singing "Faith of Our Antecedents" specifically because it pisses those people off. On the other hand, I have to remember that inclusive language includes everyone, even them. Plus I have a feeling that if you're singing a hymn just to piss someone off, you probably are and it's probably God. This is not the way to win friends and influence deities.

Another fundamental tenet of MCC is an open communion. That means anybody, even you. I still cry watching gay and lesbian couples receive the Host together. I feel so privileged coming to Christ's table to find the butch, the femme, the transgendered, the gay, the straight, and the bi. There's the African-American, Hispanic, Native American, and Asian. There's Arabian, Central American, plus exotic and wonderful blends. I'm beginning to sound like Starbucks. I suppose that would make me Vanilla Roast. My point, though, is that it's nice to *say* everyone is included—I heard that from the church I left 25 years ago in heartbreak, bitterness, and rage—but when I *see* it at MCC, I am overwhelmed and I usually cry. I think to myself, *If only I could share this with my birth family...* I believe they would cry too. I suspect for different reasons, but we're working on that.

All my life I thought tolerance was the end of the rainbow. I didn't need approval or acceptance, all I wanted was tolerance. Well, that and a live-in maid, but I was ready to

settle for tolerance. Then I walked into MCC. I was not tol-
erated, I was *celebrated.* It was like having the doors kicked
open and the walls blown down. Suddenly there was a whole
new horizon...along with a new challenge. If I am to be celebrated for what I am, I must be ready to celebrate others
just as they are—not always an easy task. I have a copy of
Ambrose Bierce's *The Devil's Dictionary,* and in it he defines
"neighbor" as "One whom we are commanded to love as
ourselves, and who does all he knows how to make us dis-
obedient." Fortunately I also have Fred to remind me how
difficult it can be to love *me.* I try to bear that in mind when
I see Mr. Helms or Mr. Falwell on TV. Hey, nobody said this
was gonna be easy.

I think that's enough to get you started if you feel like
checking out your local MCC. You don't have to dress up;
you don't even have to eat. The first time I went I had missed
breakfast and was starving. I saw coffee and muffins on a
table and thought *Hallelujah, there is a God!* And I was right,
because God is there. And after a very long, very angry, very
dry spell, God is also in my heart again. And in the person
across the street. And, despite what you may have been told,
in the person holding this book.

My favorite picture of Jesus is the one with his head
thrown back, mouth wide open laughing, you know, showing
all the dental work. I've found that kind of joy reclaiming my
spirituality as a gay man. I recommend trying it because it
feels good. It feels like healing.

A PROTEST FOR THE POST-OPERATIVE

I was late for the Solidarity With the Transgendered protest and I was wondering if I should take off my pants. Traffic hadn't moved on the 101 freeway for the last ten minutes, so I figured I could probably do it. The rally organizers asked us to bring a white T-shirt we didn't mind ruining. Some transgendered people had been brutally bashed with baseball bats at Santa Monica and La Brea the week before, so I anticipated being splashed with symbolic "blood." It was going to be very '60s and way retro, dramatic, powerful, and all that, but I didn't want anything dripping on my new jeans. Earlier in the day I had gone to a hospice thrift store in West Hollywood called Out of the Closet to get a cheap T-shirt. I'd spent over an hour selecting just the right one, simple, not too worn, more stylish than Fruit of the Loom, and under a buck. I settled on a pique knit that had the arms and bottom hem cut off and a rolled hem at the neck. Rallying with the transgendered in a rough shirt like this, I would look totally macho yet evolved. And all for 75 cents.

Traffic started moving so I postponed yanking my pants down. I would be arriving about half an hour late, but fortunately, demonstrations never start on time. For that matter, neither does anything gay. Put the two together, and I would have time to get a sex change myself. When I finally got to Santa Monica Boulevard I found a space three blocks from my church, which was sponsoring this protest. I knew the demonstration had started because the rubbernecking was already clogging Santa Monica. "Look, Marge, transeck-'shuls." Spare me.

I hopped out of the car and went around to the side away from traffic. I changed into my spotty shirt and pulled my jeans off. I reached in the backseat for my old brown cutoffs when I remembered I'd left them in the trunk. With as much dignity as one can have in BVD jockeys and gawking traffic, I went around to unlock the trunk. I looked up to see a West Hollywood sheriff glaring at me from the curb, arms crossed. "This isn't what it looks like," I said standing on Santa Monica Boulevard in Boys Town in my tightey whiteys and a trashy T-shirt. He gave me a "Shouldn't you be working the boulevard between Highland and La Brea?" look and arched an eyebrow. "Really," I said, "I just need the right shorts for the transgender protest at my church." "You're late," he grunted. There are benefits to living in a gay ghetto.

People were gathered in front of the church in their T-shirts with slogans in red ink scrawled on them, messages like STOP TRANSPHOBIA, STOP THE VIOLENCE, and I ❤ MY TRANS-GENDERED BROTHERS AND SISTERS. That last one had to be continued on the back. Disappointed there was no fake blood but anxious to blend in, I found the table with the Magic Markers. The woman there offered to write on me and asked what I wanted. I suggested STOP THE HATE. As she started, three television crews and a newspaper photographer rushed over to us to record this event for posterity. I was mortified. If I'd known I was going to be on the news, I would have bought a cleaner looking shirt. The woman writing on me was unnerved by the media attention, but she put on a good show for the cameras, even turning me around and writing PEACE NOW on my back. I felt so John Lennon. I also felt proud to be backing members of my community.

The sheriffs blocked the street for us so we could march. It is so empowering to be able to say "We want to march" and have the cops go " 'kay." This must be what straight peo-

ple feel like all the time. We shouted slogans as we walked
west on Santa Monica down to Robertson Boulevard and
back. I know I should have concentrated on the serious purpose of the march, but as these demonstrations become more
routine for me, I find my mind wandering. I wondered how
effective it was to chant slogans at the car wash we were passing. I couldn't help noticing that the boys dancing and drinking at Rage just keep getting younger and younger; they must
have child care on the premises. I also noticed I was getting
looks from one or two of the cute protesters. All right! The
shirt was working. I caught my reflection in the window of A
Different Light bookstore and really liked it. I felt so liberal,
daring, and butch, like Barbra Streisand in *Yentl* but with
more back hair. I was growing hoarse but kept shouting
because I was really getting into the husky masculine effect it
gave my voice. In a store window on the south side of the
street I saw a shirt I liked in a darling royal blue paisley and
made a mental note to come back when I had money. There
was also this killer studded belt in the window of the leather
fetish store by the church. I'd definitely have to take another
look at it after Sunday service.

The march was exhilarating. It's vitally important that we
stand together as a community and express our outrage in
highly public ways. If for no other reason than to get more
gays on TV. How dare these craven assholes attack one of my
community anyway? And yes, we are all a part of the same
community. There is a feeling, even among gays, that transgendered folk don't count for much. The not-so-funny thing
is, that's how most straights see gays—as expendable jokes. If
we treat our own the way homophobic straights treat us, we
are no better than they.

After it was over I needed to get toilet paper. This activity had no connection to the march; we were just running low
at home. I stopped at the Ralphs grocery in the Beverly
Connection. People smiled at me in my protest drag. I felt like

a living lesson in involvement on behalf of the oppressed, like Sally Field with her UNION sign in *Norma Rae*. There in the frozen foods section my shirt was the equivalent. (I know I came in for toilet paper, but I was in frozen foods because I deserved ice cream, damn it.) When another grinning stranger said, "I love your shirt," I decided to try salvaging it by dying it black. I was fishing a pint of Starbucks Mocha Java out of the freezer when I caught my reflection in the glass door. Oh. My. God. In blazing six-inch-high blood-red letters, my shirt read STOP THE HAT.

I was going to be on the 11 o'clock news protesting headwear.

"Oh, screw it," I thought. People know what I mean. Everyone can tell I have a social conscience; they just think I can't spell it. Still, I clutched the ice cream over where the E should have been, grabbed a bottle of black Rit dye, and slunk home.

The shirt came out great. I proudly showed Fred my manly, newly black, rugged memento of protest. All he said was, "How *Flashdance*," followed by, "and you forgot the toilet paper." I sulked and had seconds on ice cream.

Watching the news that night, I was happy, relieved, and disappointed. I was elated we got coverage, relieved the footage they used had me and my misspelling deep in the marching group, and disappointed that once again the trans-gendered were served up as minor freaks. Until we are none of us freaks, I'll keep marching. Of course, next time I'll buy brand new Hanes and do my own lettering.

AN MCC CHRISTMAS CAROL

As mentioned earlier, I go to the Metropolitan Community Church of Los Angeles. I love it because it is a church that constantly challenges. Especially challenging can be our theatrical versions of Bible stories. One was based on Matthew 8:5–13 wherein the Roman centurion was portrayed in full leather drag. The challenging part for me wasn't that he was in leather, but that he looked so damn good in it I had to cross my legs. But that play was nothing compared to the one about David who loved Jonathan "with a love surpassing that of women." If the Southern Baptists had seen that one, you would have heard collective jaws dropping and sphincters slamming shut with a boom like an SST leaving JFK. For those with open minds, however, the shows make their point. I find them moving. Besides, I thought David's leather tastefully restrained, especially when you consider he was a king with plenty of cows at hand.

One day in early fall I found myself having lunch at Koo Koo Roo chicken after church with Eric, the man who had written, performed, and directed the above shows. He told me he was writing a Christmas play and wanted me to be in it. As I considered the offer, I wondered what I was getting into. *Was I ready to act again? Would I have a big part? Did I own enough leather?* I asked "When are the performances?"

"December 19th and 20th," Eric said, "Saturday and Sunday."

"I always visit my folks on Christmas, usually leaving the

Saturday before. This will cut into my time with my parents," I told him. "So of course I'll do it. What's the play about?"

"It's a version of *A Christmas Carol*. You'd be playing the part of the Scrooge character's partner."

I'd done *A Christmas Carol* before. Heck, I'd written a children's musical adaptation, so I knew it intimately. "Scrooge's partner, Jacob Marley," I nodded, "I can handle that."

"No, his *partner*."

"Ah," was all I could think of to say. Of course. I should have known. I recalled the earlier plays and scorned my naïveté. I tried to get my mind around the concept of someone who would actually choose to hang out with Scrooge, let alone do the horizontal humbug. I wondered if my character had picked him up in some gay Dickensian ale house. Or did I owe him so much money he was taking it out on my arrears? And what kind of person would blow a man named Ebenezer? It was too much to think about, and besides, it was time to ask the important question.

"Who's playing Scrooge?"

"Nathan Meckley."

"Ooh!" I said. "I'm there."

Eric smiled, and I decided to press my luck.

"Are there any sex scenes?"

"No."

"Could there be?"

He looked at me, trying to decide if I was serious or not. The great thing about having a reputation as a comic is, you can be both and let the other person decide how to take it.

"Uh, no."

Hey, it was worth a shot. Anyway, it turned out our show was only loosely based on *A Christmas Carol*. I was playing a man named Steve, the partner of sad, angry Mark, who has lost a lover to AIDS and now doesn't want to go to church on Christmas Eve with Steve because he is haunted by too much guilt, grief, self-loathing, and church and family-inflicted damage from years past. What I had foreseen as a fun little church thing turned into a drama of Euripidean proportions. Rehearsals involved intense character development through improvisation. For instance, it was decided that Mark's former lover had died during December. That was a fun improv. The family had swooped in, taken the body, packed up their son's furniture, said hideous things to Mark, and left. I got to play Dad in that one. Then I got to talk about it in therapy. A lot.

We constructed several Christmases between Mark and Steve, and none of them were pretty. My character wanted to decorate like Martha Stewart on a fruitcake high. Mark wanted to crawl in a hole, and since he couldn't, he took it out on Steve. Add to this we were radical queers with, according to the script, a rainbow tree out front and Santa dressed in leather on the roof. You knew we'd get leather in there somewhere. I can only imagine their friends living in fear of getting invitations to a holiday party from these two. "Oh, no, it's an invite to another of Mark and Steve's schizo-manic Christmas dramas. Let's just send them a box of assorted cock rings and tell them we're scheduled for surgery."

The show opened with carolers singing "O Holy Night." Later Steve turns on the radio and can find only different versions, including disco, of "O Holy Night." When he's left alone in his misery he sings an ironic, gut-wrenching song about hating Christmas—to the tune of "O Holy Night." After he's discovered the meaning and joy of Christmas and decides to go to church he reprises, yes, "O Holy Night." After he finally joins Mark in the church, there's a choir concert where the finale is a gospel version of "O Holy freaking Night." Some years ago Fred and I went to a wedding in Bar Harbor, Maine. While we were there I ate lobster at every meal. Finally I ate so much of it I became ill and spent an entire afternoon throwing up. It has put me off lobster ever since. I now feel about "O Holy Night" the same way I feel about lobster.

My role in the show was a small one and, having been away from performing for years, I'm sure I was stunningly mediocre. Nevertheless, I got to kiss Nathan Meckley full on the lips twice a night in the front of a church. The real turn-on was having an audience watching me do it, but that's just my perversion. It was one of the few times I managed to browbeat Fred into coming to church, which is always the best way to get someone to attend. He had a grand time laughing at my performance for all the wrong reasons. He didn't laugh at the kissing, though. Ho ho ho.

The rest of the audience were exceedingly polite to me afterward, saying those things you say when trapped into expressing counterfeit praise. "No one else could have done what you did with that role." "Your performance was truly memorable." And my favorite, "You did so much with such a small part." Unfortunately, I sometimes hear that one elsewhere.

All in all it was a terrific experience and raised several hundred dollars for the church. So now I'm wondering what Eric's Christmas show is going to be this year. *Frosty the Leatherman*? *Santa Claus is Coming to Top*? *The Little Drummer Magazine Boy*? I'm sure it'll be interesting, challenging, fun, and somehow involve cowhide. I'll be sitting front and center unless Eric suffers a lack of memory and casts me again. On the other hand, I'd love to be part of something like *How Master Grinch Stole Christmas*. I can see it now.

All the Whos down in Whoville wanted handcuffs and got 'em
But still were not happy, for Whos are all bottoms.

I guarantee you I'll be looking forward to the improv for that.

LOOKING FOR GAY PRIDE
AT THE GAY PRIDE FESTIVAL

If it's June, the Los Angeles Gay Pride Festival can't be far off, and every year it seems it's more about making a buck and less about pride. I asked a friend of mine whether he was going to the festival and he said, "No, I already have a bank and a phone service, what's the point?" I know how he feels. It's rough paying a $15 festival entry fee for the privilege of purchasing overpriced rainbow tchotchkes and T-shirts you can't wear anywhere else. Still, I believe there remains a huge element of pride. Like my flabby body, it just needs a little better definition.

Let's start by defining what pride is not. Pride does not come from being sponsored by beer companies or radio stations. No one comes to a sense of pride passing through tents pitching personal lubricants either. What you can be proud of is that enough of us have come out of the closet to make up a demographic worth pursuing. If every gay person came out, advertisers would drool over the numbers like I drool over Brush Creek Media's star bear Jack Radcliffe. Suddenly tight-ass companies would be after that queer dollar faster than you can say "Ikea." Imagine seeing gays getting potted gardenias and lesbians lining up to buy paint in a Wal-Mart ad. It could happen. You could help. Take a rainbow mug to work.

Pride is not putting on your fetish wear—and that includes what passes for gym togs—and prancing about one weekend a year. Don't get me wrong, I am extremely pro-prance and recommend it. I believe if more straight people let go and pranced, we'd all enjoy each other more and stop being so warlike. I prance every chance I get, but prancing at the festival is fun, not pride. True, your personal expression is a part of pride, but expressing yourself one measly weekend out of 52 (OK, two weekends out of 52, I forgot Halloween) does not make up pride. If, however, you have the self assurance to know you are *entitled* to prance *every single day* of the whole damn year, that, honey, is pride.

It's important to know that pride does not come from simply being gay either. Please, if that were all it took, there'd be a lot more therapists out of work. We also wouldn't be treating each other like Southern Baptists treat Disney. It pisses me off that there are homos who shun drag queens, leather boys, the transgendered, motorcycle dykes, and other parts of our community who "go too far." They've got their PC panties in a wad over how we'll be portrayed in the media if "those people" are allowed to be seen. I've got news for you: The media would portray us badly if we were dressed like Mormons on Sunday, so screw 'em. We've got to accept each other first if we ever expect to be accepted by the rest of the world. Like the song says, "We are family, I've got all my sisters with me." What part of "all" don't you understand?

So where do I find pride in our community? It is in the journey each of us took in overcoming the lies, degradation, and damage done to us. "I walked into the dining room," one man told me, "and said 'Dad, I'm gay, and either that frosted plastic chandelier goes or I go.' Seems they wanted the Liberace look more than they wanted a son, so, hello, West Hollywood, here I am." A lesbian friend gave me this account of coming out: "My stepdad knocked over a chair and shouted at me to get out of the house for good right then or he'd beat me worse than ever. That was such a no-brainer, my straight brother jumped up said he was queer so he could get the hell out too. A month later my straight sister did the same thing. My stepdad started to catch on, though, when my mother told him she was a lesbertarian." That we can laugh at the ugliness is a testament to the mighty strength of our spirit. There's one helluva cause for pride. Pink triangle pins for everyone!

We each have our stories. I'm proud I slogged through my hell, and I'm proud I'm still making it because it remains an ongoing journey. Sometimes it's smooth sailing; other times it feels like I'm in steerage on the *Titanic*. That wounded, outraged, and angry people can come together not in violence but in a party so big they have to block off major streets in a world-class city is a fucking miracle. You want something else to be proud of? There it is, baby. We're treated like dirt and we still we show the world how to party. And, while we're at it, how to dress, dance, decorate, cook, cater, eat, sing, paint, sculpt, write, smell, accessorize, put on a show, and work with leather. Damn it, if not for us, the Pacific Design Center in West Hollywood would look like the softer side of Sears and Madonna would be on VH1's *Where Are They Now?* That's power. When you can come through the shit we have and smell like Le Male by Gaultier you have every reason to be proud, girlfriend.

I am also proud of every single G, L, B, and T who has learned to say "screw it all" and embraced their own worth because, believe me, that positive force benefits not only them but everyone, whether you "do it" with men, women, or seasonal melons. I am doubly proud of those who have come through it who are now helping others make their way. When you speak to queer youth you're like Ernest Borgnine in *The Poseidon Adventure* swimming back for the others—only probably not as hairy. And if you are, send me dirty Polaroids and keep up the good work.

That's why I can put up with the booths at the festival peddling everything from porno to piercings, home loans to harnesses, corn on the cob to cock rings. I can even take the inevitable T-shirts that say "I'm not a lesbian but my 27 cats are." It's because the festival is an opportunity to see and be seen in all our diverse butch, femme, hairy, shaven, portly, buffed, natural, vegan, uptight and/or bare-assed 24/7 glory. Buy an ice cream cone, sit down, and just watch the crowd roll by. We are every size and shape, every color and creed. Look how amazing we are. And look at how many of us there are. Wouldn't Fred Phelps just shit? Gay pride is a chance to look into each others' eyes to see the strength within ourselves and to recognize the power we carry as a people.

This pride festival, go out and fight for a parking space. Overpay to leave your car in somebody's driveway or break down and take the bus. Just get there. Once a year you need to see what there is to be proud of. And that's you, sweetheart. Hundreds of thousands of you.

Dress accordingly.

PART FIVE
Food and Sex

FOOD & WINE & PORNO

Like any normal gay man, I have my stash of porn. I have videos, magazines, and photos, but there's one thing that really kneads my dough, beats my batter, toasts my walnuts, creams my corn, and drains my dumplings. It's *Food & Wine* magazine. Every dish is as perfect as a Colt model and portrayed with a sensuality about as subtle as an International Male catalog. It's put out by American Express Publishing, but it's every bit as obscene as anything from Old Reliable Video.

Food & Wine is like porno in so many ways. For instance, they just assume I have a kugelhoph mold. That's like the video I have (in 3-D no less) that assumes I have an interest in learning massage. And just as this tape requires special equipment to get the full effect, one needs a food processor to make almost every recipe *F&W* prints. That hinders me because I don't do well with any machine smarter than a hand mixer, but that doesn't mean I can't look at the pictures of Roquefort-Walnut Terrines With Apple Salad and drool. After all, I do the same thing to photos of Steve Kelso. So what if I can't make Roasted Duck With Licorice-Merlot Sauce, I won't be making Mr. Kelso either. I mean, come on, how many perfect porn stars have you peeled, filled, and served up with a warm beurre blanc? I even regard my *F&W* collection of past favorite issues as highly as I regard my Kelso calendars, 1995–2000 inclusive, thank you. I pull them out when I'm by myself, and they give me that special feeling I need when only fantasy will do. Yes, yes, Curried

Scallops on Pumpkin Polenta Cakes. Oh, God, *yes*!

Sometimes the pages even get sticky, but then you try making Pears Poached in Spiced Red Wine without getting it everywhere in the excitement. I had to try them because there was no food processor involved and there's nothing I enjoy more than a good pear in my mouth. (Say it out loud, dear.)

If Fred's in the other room, he can't tell which I'm looking at. Was it an issue of *Inches* or an article on picnicking in Provence that caused me to comment "Nice basket"? When I mumbled "What a spread," was it over the four-color foldout for Wedgewood china or Tom Katt getting ready to make another friend? Was I looking at a photo of Chinese peasants harvesting back-breaking amounts of Darjeeling when I said "That's a big load" or was I watching *Powertool*? Again.

In both cases it's about glorious extremes. Just recently *F&W* gushed that they had found a place that will mail you a chocolate pound cake that arrives with an "exquisite nosegay atop the cake." It comes in an enormous hatbox made of embossed velvet. That is as over-the-top as any of the deliciously indecent debauchery served up by Tom of Finland, and for me, it's at least as gratifying. I once found myself ogling gossamer Venetian glassware by Christofle which *F&W* had the temerity to call "whimsical." At $350 a *stem*! It's pure grocery store get-off material.

In an article on kitchen makeovers *F&W* insists "the pull-out has to be stable and strong; the quality of the hardware is crucial." I could swear I read the same thing in producer-director Chi Chi LaRue's book *Making It Big: Sex Stars, Porn Films, and Me*. Indeed, the further one goes, the more difficult it becomes to tell them apart. I'll prove it to you with this simple test. Below are a few quotes. I defy you to tell me which are from *F&W* and which are from *Making It Big*:

"This is something that's not to everyone's taste, but I just adore it."

"One...isn't enough.... I have three, so there's one every-where you turn. Two are for trash."

"Boy...if you could do that with a wine bottle, you'd save a whole lot of grief."

"It's better to mix it up. Go fast and hard for a while, then try slow and easy."

"You get a nice pop and that same satisfied feeling."

The similarities go on and on. *Food & Wine* thinks I can waltz into the corner grocery and come out with pancetta and haricots verts. It's equally as likely that Hank Hightower will waltz into my bedroom and come out with a smile and matted chest hair. *F&W* lists the best establishments for wine by city. It's like a *Damron Guide* for oenophiles. In one issue they described a 1997 Cos d'Estournel Bordeaux as "charm-ing, graceful, yet intensely endowed." One could say the same for Zak Spears. They gave an award to a man who invented a new kind of wine bottle cork. The video industry gives awards to men who invent new ways of popping other men's corks.

The point is, sensuous images arouse sensual desires, whether in food or foreplay. And it's not only enjoyable, but educational. I can state with absolute conviction that it was the combination of *Food & Wine* magazine and Brush Creek Media's *Bear Trackers* that taught me everything I know about outdoor entertaining. So if you come over for a picnic, honey, bring plenty of napkins.

MEN IN BLACK

What is it about men in leather? I don't know, I'm asking. I've just discovered Vietnamese food, and I mourn the years I spent without it. I'd hate to discover at my age (none of your business, thank you) that leather fits into that same category. Could I have a whole new fetish awaiting me? One that replaces Häagen-Dazs?

I had to start somewhere, so I went to my local adult toy store, the Pleasure Chest, asking questions that caused what I felt to be excessive eye-rolling. "Does this come in something other than black?" "Is this a wristband? It seems a tad small" And what appeared to be a staff favorite: "What if somehow something, well…spills on it?" The clerks stifled their laughter and showed me jackets, vests, shorts, long pants, belts, chaps, shoes, boots, collars, armbands, hoods, and about 200 kinds of harnesses. I already loved leather! It was all about shopping! Or so I thought until I checked out the magazines. "Ee-e-eek!"

And then "Oo-o-oh!" Which I think pretty much captures the appeal, at least for this beginner. *Oh, dear God, this poor man in the picture!* I thought. *How barbaric! How disgusting! How much is this magazine?* Clearly leather was about embracing the forbidden and finding freedom therein. Something I'd only dabbled in with Oreos. I felt new horizons calling and left with an armband, hat, jacket, boots, various "literature," and the certainty I had exceeded my Visa limit, but I didn't care. I was already learning that pain can be good.

Which was fortunate because it was 97° outside, and wearing all that cowhide home was punishment indeed. Fortunately, being gay, I don't have a problem enduring pain for the sake of fashion. Not only that, but by the time I got home I'd lost three pounds.

Purely on impulse, I'd also picked up a ticket to the Tom of Finland bash in Hollywood. What was I getting myself into? According to the ticket we were supposed to have "leather, muscles, and sweat." I could only muster two out of the three. It also said, "We encourage you to indulge your fantasies," and I had a feeling they weren't talking about the one I have where Patti LuPone cleans my house while I sing selections from *Evita*. I know leather people are very serious about their lifestyle, and I didn't want to embarrass anyone (least of all myself) so I went to A Different Light bookstore, where I bought *Leathersex* by Joseph W. Bean and *Ties That Bind* by Guy Baldwin. (I also purchased *Boy Wonder: My Life in Tights* by Burt Ward because leather might turn out to be a passing thing with me, but celebrity trash is forever.) I already liked *Leathersex* by the third paragraph: "Tell the man or men you are with that you are a novice. Tell him (them) what you think you want…" Plural partners! Who doesn't love a party?

Mr. Bean and Mr. Baldwin each give excellent information while shying away from nothing. I admired their frankness, especially in areas many people are unwilling even to consider, like water sports, processing pain, and fisting. "Please stop telling me about this," begged a friend. "I can actually feel my penis withdrawing into my body. I'm getting an inverse erection." I remember thinking, *This from a man with a thing for Tim Conway*.

Leather is a willingness to explore, to fantasize, to consider taboos not as a boundary but as a door to possible pleasures. How do you know you don't like the mango mint surprise if you won't even taste it? I studied my books. I learned about the joys of spanking and remembered Billy Blevins in third grade, who always seemed to invite meetings with the "board of education." After a paddling he would come back to his seat with a wet, red face and a smirk I suddenly understood. I read about the role of spandex in bondage, and will never view the ladies shopping at the Glendale Galleria in quite the same way. I perused the information on slave abuse, thinking if I could turn getting my bathroom clean into a kinky experience for someone, this was for me. Then, with a start, I realized *I* could be the one forced to suffer the abusive discipline of cleaning my filthy toilet. That's when I knew I would be wearing my armband on the right.

It was the day of the Tom of Finland do, and I still didn't feel I was "getting it" so I called all my friends who were into leather. Over and over I heard it was the smell, the feel, the look, the attitude. That didn't help. It sounded like a Polo ad. There was nothing to be done but get dressed, go to Hollywood, and experience it for myself.

Wow. Nothing could have prepared me for walking into the middle of hundreds of men shed of inhibitions and most of their clothes. There were various demonstrations of consensual physical abuse, verbal abuse, and self-abuse. Hot wax, bondage, flogging, fire, shaving—and that was just getting to the bar. There was the man wearing only boots who was content to be led around by a leash connected to his Prince Albert. I was also impressed by a man wearing only a leather apron who would piss on your boots and then buff them for that special high gloss look. The amazing thing to me was that all night long he never ran out of piss. There was another gentleman who buried his head in my chest while he did what the monkeys were doing the last time I visited the zoo. Far from being offended, I encouraged him—until I spilled some very cold beer at an inopportune moment and he moved on. In one visit to the rest room I made more friends than in my entire junior year at college. The entire event was thick with masculine sexuality, close, sweaty bodies, and lascivious displays of aggressive abandon. It was appalling, it was shocking, and it was over *way* too soon.

So what did I learn? One: Spilled poppers can leave a red place for days. Two: The leather scene has to be experienced to be understood. It may not be for you, but you won't know unless you're open to experimenting with something new. I know I experienced only a party, not the lifestyle, but it's a titillating start. Remember, the journey of a thousand miles begins with a single step—and now I not only have the right boots, but they have a shine you can't get most places.

CRUISING—Looking for Love in all the Lit Places

Having a life partner keeps one from roaming the sexual rounds. Oh, sure there's been that odd dash to the spa, but other than that we really don't go looking. Still, there are those nonbar places where, well, things just happen. And don't look so shocked; one likes to know one still has it, even if one is not giving it away. So for those interested in places to cruise other than clubs, let me tell you what I've found.

Bed Bath & Beyond is terrific, especially if, like me, you find it difficult to start conversation. You can turn to almost any customer and say, "Hi, I'm serving cantaloupe tonight. Would you say I needed a good baller?" Bed Bath & Beyond is absolutely filled to the rafters with all sorts of shiny, baffling things, so simply grab a clerk—and at the store in the Beverly Center, trust me, it can be *any* clerk—and start asking. "Could you explain the lofting properties of various goose down pillow fill...and tell me what you sleep with?" Play your cards right and you can skip the Bed, skip the Bath, and get right to that big, bad, bouncing Beyond.

You say you like the all-American, wide-eyed, apple-pie type? Three words: Main Street, Disneyland. These boys are practically wearing signs. If you like that Up-With-People thing, just sidle up to the register with a Tarzan plush toy, smile, and ask, "Where can I find one of these after hours?" Even if it's a straight boy who fell through the cracks (yeah, right), there's nothing they can do, so flirt away. They have to stay friendly, or Disney will kill their families.

A friend of mine told me the airport is a good place, especially the areas around those shuttle flights to San Francisco. I don't know how or where he does what I can only assume he's doing, but he always smiles like he's had that "something special in the air." I hate him.

Trendoid areas like Melrose Avenue are cruisy if you're into piercing and comic-book hair colors. I'm not, but I always wondered just how far down those dye jobs went. As for the piercing I go both ways—the pros are that you know where you are in the dark and they're handy little knobs to twist; the con is that they are often just something to knock one's teeth against. Anyway, there's tons of these radical queers out there, and given how skinny most of them are, you get lots and lots per ton. Just be aware that for the most part they are very young. It probably helps if you have your own skateboard and acne.

Pavilions grocery in West Hollywood is where gay professionals of a certain age pick up their flowers, Tanqueray, and party boys. Everyone is well-mannered, overpackaged, and far too pretty yet somehow discretely understated. Don't let that fool you. Sex is as readily available as the take-out panini and only slightly less crusty. A word of warning, though: Due to the hierarchy of money, muscles, and Lycra wear, you enter this grocery AYOR. I was clearly out of my league strolling the aisles in 36-30 Dockers with a cart full of MET-Rx Bars and Chips Ahoy, fooling no one. To hell with Pavilions. In the produce section at Hughes Market in Silver Lake men eye each other while hefting zucchini and loose carrots with no subtlety whatsoever. I've seen torrid looks exchanged between people at the checkout that told me the Ben & Jerry's was never going to make it home to the freezer in time. It is shockingly overt, like a sex club, only with fluorescent lighting and cat food. Two weeks before Christmas I was in the dairy section, where I overheard a conversation involving words like "creamy," "thick," and "sweet." They were not discussing eggnog.

Hardware stores in gay areas are better than any grocery store, especially if you like that Mr. Fix-It kind of guy (or gal, for that matter), and I do love a man who's good with his hands. One morning in the hardware store on Santa Monica at San Vicente I saw, I swear to god, the Brawny Paper Towel man. He was bent over in tight, low-slung painters pants digging through a bin of, well, I don't know, *stuff*. To me, hardware stores are filled with widgets, gizmos, and thingummys, butch items that are both mysterious and intimidating. I wasn't going to let that stop me, though. I went right over with the best line I could come up with. "Doing tool-type jobbies?" I said, wincing as I heard it fall out of my mouth. He stood up, towering over me. He smiled dazzlingly. I had to clutch a nearby display of whing-dings for balance.

"Yeah," he said in a deep voice, resonating in a large chest brimming with hair. "I just ripped out a wall."

"My God, a whole wall!" I babbled in near-falsetto, "and it isn't even 10 o'clock!" In case you don't know, babbling in near-falsetto is a major cruising "don't." He wrinkled his nose, responded rather pointedly that his *wife* wanted the renovations, and turned away. Wife, yeah. With a yellow hankie in his left pocket. Who needs *that,* anyway? Or at any rate before 10 o'clock? On second thought, hardware stores are the worst.

Better to check out the local Laundromat. Where else can you legitimately start off a conversation with "Wow, nice basket," and end with "Boy, did you ever have a big load!" You also get to see if it's boxers or briefs (and exactly how brief), and even get some idea of what they're into. At our old apartment in Silver Lake we shared a washer with a neighbor who was into fisting. If you're not into that and the person you're approaching has no children but is doing diapers, you might want to rethink.

By now you should have a couple of new ideas of where

to do your cruising. Basically, anywhere people gather and linger is where you want to be: furniture stores, restaurants, airports, bus stations, rest stops, the second-floor men's room in the Robinsons-May at Santa Monica Place mall. Oops, I mean, so I'm told. So, what are you doing? Put down this book, get out there, and start the dance!

FOOD TO GO

When I was a young child, whenever our family went on road trips and we stopped someplace iffy, my father would order the only things he deemed safe: hard-boiled eggs and bottled Coke. Our yearly excursion to our cousins was a seven-hour ordeal through squalid towns on U.S. 1. That meant, thanks to Dad's safety menu, the car was ripe with sulfur from lunch on and the first day at our cousins' was spent in the bathroom. I swore from then on that I would eat whatever the locals had to offer no matter where I went.

One of my favorite things about traveling is the food. God knows I'm not talking about the food you eat while doing the traveling, I mean the food you eat when you get there. I've learned to take food with me on any flight that lasts longer than it would take to get a perm. On an 11-hour flight to England the airline served sandwiches with all the flavor of communion wafers and just as filling. Thank goodness I'd bought a banana in the airport and stuck it in my pocket for later. Of course, after I took it out, the steward who'd been flirting with me lost all interest.

We touched down at Heathrow and already I was looking forward to toad-in-the-hole, bubble-and-squeak, and other *Masterpiece Theatre*–type dishes, even though we had been told the food in England would be bad. The truth is, it wasn't bad. It was much, much worse. The British don't cook their food so much as render it helpless. It was all boiled, fried, or mashed to a pasty, pulpy muck. In desperation we went to a

Pizza Hut, thinking, *How can you screw up pizza?* Well, the British are a thorough people. As an experiment, Fred chewed on the box and found it indistinguishable from the contents. No wonder the British built an empire. They had no choice but to conquer other countries that actually had cuisines and bring them home. Once we discovered this, we had delicious Indonesian, Thai, and Indian meals. We didn't even mind when they repeated on us because it was still better than what we had been eating earlier.

On a flight to Athens we were served a poorly thought out breakfast of rice with milk, raisins, and olives. I made it to the hotel just in time for the food poisoning to kick in. When I finally ventured out two days later it was with a very queasy stomach. I tottered into a taverna where I ordered the only thing I could translate: calamari, expecting soothing, anonymous little fried rings. I was presented with an enormous whole roasted squid. The glistening white body covered the plate, the tentacles running off across the table. I forced myself to take a bite. It was terrific, and I ate every last sucker. At another meal the suckers on the marinated octopus, being much bigger, presented a different problem. Does one eat them or put them aside? I decided to go for it. They were chewy, but I've had clams at Howard Johnsons that were more work to eat.

When in France I had sweet meats—and for the uninitiated, they are neither sweet nor meat...exactly—but everything I ate there was nothing less than superb. I had escargot stew, frog legs, even horse, all delicious. I got to the point where if I had seen *merde* on the menu, I'd have said, "Bring me another double vodka and I'll try it." Also, every meal seemed to end with a cheese plate. For Fred it was all variations on a theme of runny and stinky. I, however, couldn't get enough. Of course that meant brushing my teeth thoroughly before getting any Fred.

Switzerland is where you go if you have too much money

and need to be cured of that. What I paid for chocolate in Geneva could have kept me in quality porno for months. Then again, the chocolate was so good, it had the same effect. Restaurants were so expensive, we drove around Lake Geneva back into France to eat in Evian, where they tried to get us to order bottled water. We didn't fall for that. Even if it's coming out of the tap it's Evian water, right?

On a cruise ship the dining is fabulous and the entrées are sinfully abundant. "I'm done with my steak; take it away and bring me the lobster." Then, "I'm done with my lobster; take it away and bring me the chicken, the swordfish, *and* the fettuccine primavera." I wanted it all in front of me at the same time. I couldn't eat it but I could roll in it.

On this cruise we stopped at the fabulous and highly scenic world-famous resort town of Ensenada, where we were warned not to eat or drink anything in town. From street vendors I bought the most scrumptious fish taco and lemonade I've ever had. The only side effect I had was recurring dreams of the hunky lemonade man wherein I juiced his lemons and served him beef burritos. We don't need to go too deeply into that.

On a trip to Laughlin, Nev., a few years ago the only meals we could afford after our luck at the slots were cheap-ass buffets. Nothing was fresh. Everything was steamed to death and swimming in oily butter. We ate the garnish and called it salad.

Visiting Jacksonville, Fla., we saw a billboard on the way in from the airport proclaiming a local steak house as "Home of the Big Fat Yeast Roll!" Doesn't that just make you want to skip lunch so you can arrive hungry? Our first night in town we went to Woody's Barbecue, a local chain, where you can get a glorious mess of a barbecue sandwich with lots of sauce. Do I have to tell you it was called a "Sloppy Woody?" And at $3.95 what a bargain! In L.A. a sloppy woody costs $15, and that's just for a locker. While we were in Orlando we saw a brochure for the "Pirate Dinner Adventure," a sort of a Medieval Times in dry dock. We had to go. As part of our "Pirate Feast" we got "Matey Rolls and Butter." We wondered if that was "Matey Butter," and if so, did they need kitchen volunteers?

Next week I will be visiting my parents on the North Carolina coast and I'm already salivating. This is the land of golden hush puppies, fresh deep-fried seafood, and absolutely amazing chopped barbecue you don't want to inspect too closely. If you're ever there, make sure you taste the local food. And if the barbecue makes you squeamish, there's always boiled eggs and bottled Coke.

THE "HOW READY ARE YOU?" COMMITMENT TEST

Some of us are made for monogamy; some of us are made to be passed around at parties like the crudest of crudités. It might be a good idea to get a handle on where you stand before opening that joint bank account. I know whereof I speak because I am in a committed relationship that, thus far, has lasted 19 years. That not only makes me an expert, it makes me smug. But how are you to know if you are better suited for homemaking or home wrecking? Easy, grab a pencil and take the following test. If you're already in a relationship, this will give you an indication of where you stand. Remember, no cheating, at least not while you're taking the test.

You're at the checkout in the grocery when you notice your significant other cruising the bag boy.
(a) You decide to beg your boyfriend not to do that.
(b) You decide to bag your own groceries.
(c) You decide to bag your boyfriend.

Your significant other cannot name one movie starring Bette, Barbra, or Liza.
(a) You show him your movie collection to educate him.
(b) You show disappointment but feel you can work it out with counseling.
(c) You show him back to his wife and children.

Your significant other mentions the possibility of a holy union ceremony.

(a) You leave to get fitted for matching tuxes and book a honeymoon suite in Vermont.

(b) You leave.

(c) You leave skid marks.

He wants to vacation in the mountains; you want to vacation at the shore.

(a) You go to the mountains this year and the shore next year.

(b) The two of you compromise, going somewhere neither wants to go.

(c) You talk it out so he is OK with going to the mountains by himself. Then you clean out the bank account, change your name, go to Key West, and never come back.

You want vegetarian pizza; he wants sausage. He orders. When the pizza boy arrives, it's sausage.

(a) You keep the pizza, but tell him next time you'll be ordering and it will not be sausage.

(b) You throw him out but keep the pizza, even though it is sausage.

(c) You throw him and the pizza out but keep the pizza boy. And his sausage.

He forgets your birthday.

(a) You forgive him because, after all, you didn't tell him how important it was to you.

(b) You make life hell for him for weeks until, out of self-preservation and guilt, he buys you something fabulous.

(c) You cut up his clothes, throw out his CDs, mail intimate Polaroids of the two of you to his family and boss, call TRW to ruin his credit, put sugar in his gas tank, turn the oven on high, and leave. Hey, tit for tat, right?

You come home to find your significant other in bed with the pool boy.

(a) You recognize this as a symptom of a relationship in trouble and suggest couples counseling.

(b) You recognize that the relationship is over and create a scene so operatic and ugly that you lead on the 11 o'clock news.

(c) You recognize the pool boy from the tearoom at the mall and tell him to move over in bed.

You argue constantly about money.

(a) Together you agree to go see a financial consultant.

(b) You scream and yell at each other until one of you gives in and finally gets a job.

(c) While he's at work you sell everything in the house and buy Lotto tickets.

He suggests that you should work out at the gym.

(a) You don't work out at the gym. Instead, hurt, you go to Baskin-Robbins and work your way through all 31 flavors.

(b) You work out at the gym.

(c) You work the steam room at the gym.

Your significant other calls to say he's going to be working late. Again.

(a) You accept it because love means trust.

(b) You lovingly whip up his favorite meal and surprise him with it at work—just to make sure.

(c) You roll over and tell Raul you've got time for another go-round.

SCORING:
Give yourself ten points for every time you answered (a), five for each (b), and zero for each (c).
100 to 95 points: A near-perfect score! You are over-

whelmingly needy, clingy, and desperate. You make me really nervous. Get therapy.

90 to 55 points: OK, this is more like it. You are ready to enter a one-on-one relationship, but you're not so nutsy that you don't recognize the benefit of an occasional "piece of strange."

50 to 30 points: You're not at the ideal stage to be entering a relationship now. If you are already living with someone, keep the lease in your name. If the lease is in his name, co-opt his pet. It won't cushion the fall, but it'll sure piss him off.

25 to 5 points: You're not ready, and you're fooling yourself if you think you are. Any relationship you are in is doomed, futile, over, and, in short, a pathetic pile of ashes. Do the other person a favor and just go. Leave a hundred bucks on the dresser. That'll make him feel better.

0 points: You're a slut. You're looser than Liz Taylor in *Butterfield 8*. Not only are you way wrong for a relationship, you are the original good time had by all. There's nothing shameful about that unless you are my ex, who was working his way through every store manager at the mall while I was at home lovingly pasting photos of our trip to Mexico into photo albums. (Really, Brad, the guy from *Thom McAn*?)

For what it's worth, Fred and I have fallen into all of the above categories at one time or another in our relationship. If you can fight your way back to the higher scores, you stand a pretty good chance of enduring. You just have to commit to the fight. Now you know why those folks in relationships spend so much time fighting. Enjoy!

EXTREMELY PERSONAL ADS

I'm hanging out at the house and Fred is away on business and I'm bored, so naturally I turn to the personal ads at the back of one of California's better gay rags. I'm not looking to buy, but I do enjoy shopping. Especially when there are pictures. Still, there seems something ominous about men advertising for sex but not showing their faces. It's as if they're saying, "I've got a killer bod but a mug like a southbound baboon." The few who do show their faces are so over-the-top serious it's a total turnoff. Someone really needs to tell them to relax. It's sex, people, not an audit—although some aspects may be similar.

Some of the photos are so enticing, they hardly need words. Carl shows his amazing torso with only the message, "What you want in a masseur." Given what I'm seeing, what I want in a masseur is me. Another man, Josh, wears a microscopic thong and offers a full-body massage, "Mostly out." I understand, Josh. When I wear a thong I'm mostly out, too.

I enjoyed the ad headlined "Straight Guy." How straight can he be if he's advertising in the man-to-man section of a queer magazine? He describes himself as "A real guy! 5 feet 10 inches, 185, handsome, musc. ex-N.Y. cop." I have a friend in Manhattan who twice a week meets up with a New York cop who has a wife and kids in Staten Island. My friend told me the cop wanted to take him to a motel in Jersey and piss on him. I told my friend I thought that was disgusting. You can do that in Manhattan.

There's one guy I'd like to meet because he has fun ads all over the personals section. I don't want to have sex with him, but I wouldn't mind having coffee. His ads state his name and have a follow-up line that's just a calculated howler: "Gus. Pee-nuttier!" "Gus. Got milked?" "Gus. The incredible edible leg!" OK, so he's reaching, but there's no one else showing any humor, and that alone puts him over the top in my book. Most of the ads are numbingly direct, like the one with a phone number and only the words "Lick Butt, Bo." That's not sex, it's a village in Vietnam.

There's another Bo who advertises his phone number, display pager, E-mail address, Web site, and fan club. Fan club? Well, I'm told Bo is a porn star, so I guess it's understandable. Knowing that, though, I now have *Mommie Dearest* images of Bo yelling at his assistant, Caroline, who is signing his 8-by-10 glossies. "What do you mean we've run out? I must tell Catalina Video to send more! Christina, *bring me the fax!*"

Maybe if I weren't a writer the following ad wouldn't be such a total woodkill: "I'm dead straight"—which is two strikes against him already—"& one of the most handsomest in the land. If your sexually wise thru practice & grant an offer I cannot refuse I maybe prepared to undergo letting you break in my hard worked out body." This is like seeing one of those guys at the bar who gives you a chubby from across the room, so you adjust yourself and go over. Then he opens his big stupid mouth, and you realize there's that library book you urgently need to return.

Speaking of literature, do we really have to drag Herman Melville into this? Witness Matt's headline, "Moby Dick." Really, Matt, could we think of nothing else?

How about E.B. White's *One Man's Meat*? Or perhaps Saul Bellow's *Dangling Man*? Come on, show a little resourcefulness. Alas, Matt's next ad will probably read, "Long Day's Journey Into Your Butt."

Not that there aren't ads with literary quality. I particularly like this one from Ron:

> Nine inches, uncut.
> UB hung hot leather top.
> Eat out my hot ass.

It's simple, eloquent, and to the point. What are the odds Ron knows this is a haiku?

Here's an ad that took me back to my childhood:

> Big Black Dick
> Long, hard, thick.
> Total topman. Call me. Rick.

Not only is it erotic, it's Dr. Seuss.

With some of these guys, I can't help but wonder if they know what they're saying when they place their ads. "Brian, fat and thick." That would describe my ex-boss, his wife, and most of their children. "Massage from bearded BB, has table with muscular arms." Well, I suppose if his table went to the gym often enough...

Along the same lines, a man named Max has a picture ad headlined, "Total stud with mushroom head." I know what he means, but the photo shows his body from the neck down so it appears he's ashamed of the head above his shoulders. Perhaps he is. Maybe the reason he announces his tragic skull in such large letters is so there won't be any surprises—"My God, your head!"—when he comes to your door.

Another interesting phenomenon is that only men with one-syllable names seem to advertise. Max, Matt, Carl, Rick, Gus, Bo, Nick, Vince, Dave, Brad, Mike. One Elliot. The occasional Paulo. But where are the longer names? You never see "Great rim jobs by Bartholomew." "Hot cock worship from Algernon." "Shoot your sexy man-load with Zebadiah." I guess multiple-syllable names just don't have the same sound.

I was nearing the end of the section when I saw where Scott was advertising "Leatherman, Cowboy, CHiP, Const. Wkr., Marine." Throw in "Indian," and he's the Village People. Any man with this many outfits is not into sex half as much as he's into shopping. Scott, I'd much rather go to a mall with you than to bed.

I closed the magazine. I was still bored, but what to do? I'd have to tidy the house first if I was actually going to call one of these guys. I don't care if they know I'm a slut, but I can't have them thinking I'm messy. And if they did come over there'd be sheets, rugs, and curtains to clean afterwards. (I like to get my money's worth.) So I decided to take a cue from monosyllabically monikered Scott and go shopping. Explaining the Visa bill is a lot easier than explaining marks on my back or why the sofa bed won't close. Besides, if I don't like what I get, I can always take it back. Try doing that with a case of the clap.

ONE MAN'S FOOD

I look at going into a grocery store as a battle to get out with the most food for the least money. I enter with sale items memorized and a thick stack of coupons. I compare prices and read labels. I am a sensible shopper and an aware consumer, and it all goes out the window when Fred comes along.

Fred is the love of my life and a joy to know. He is also a food packager's wet dream. When he sees a bright and shiny can of Pillsbury Cinnamon Rolls With Icing or a beckoning box of Ritz Bits Sandwiches, his eyes glaze over like Tastykakes. No amount of "But this is half the price of that" works. His is a force against which I am powerless, and I must resign myself to the fact that I will not be paying cash this trip.

Fred likes food that is fun. That includes anything with "Pockets," "Pouches," or "Toaster" in the name. And it has to sound jolly to make or eat: Cheese Poppers, Snack Wraps, Bagel Bites. Apostrophes and silly spellings increase the fun quotient. The very kicky Dippin' Stix had both, so he bought two boxes. Anything with "'n" in the middle like Shake 'n Bake or Brown 'n Serve, and he's out of control. We have two cats and he still tries to buy Kibbles 'n Bits.

A can of frosting is way fun. "How?" I ask, struggling to understand. "It just sits there in the can." As if explaining to a child, he tells me, "Frosting is fun because you can put it on anything and it improves everything." If somebody invents a product called Toast 'n Poppin' Fun Stix 'n Frosting, I'll never see him again.

Fred is also a sucker for the current campaign of making food cute by making it small. He adores small. Frozen petite quiches, buffalo chicken wings, mini Babybel cheeses. In a perfect world Fred would live on appetizers and croutons. I have to remember it was Fred who came up with the Small Diet. On the Small Diet you can eat whatever you want as long as it sounds small: Baby Ruth, Junior Mints, Little Debbies. And we buy them all.

I blame Kraft for this trend in tiny and twee. The world was perfectly happy with regular sized marshmallows until Kraft foisted Jet-Puffed Miniatures on us in the '60s. Then Nabisco got in on the act by making their horse-choking bales of Shredded Wheat "spoon-sized." You can just hear the marketing meetings: "Sir, our research indicates we could sell more Oreos if our cookies were cuter." "Well, how do we do that?" "By making them itty-bitty. Lab results prove that at precisely one-half inch around, the Oreo becomes quantifiably darling. And there's an even more amazing finding. With only slightly altered packaging we can call it *cereal*."

For Fred, some foods fall into the nostalgia category. Wonder Bread, Pop-Tarts, Hostess fruit pies. "Ooh! Corn dogs on a stick!" he wistfully crooned as he lovingly placed a frozen three-pound box in the cart. He was upset that Franco-American had taken their classic SpaghettiOs and made them into, among other things, Where's Waldo pasta. He wasn't sure he wanted to find Waldo or any part of him in his pasta and sauce.

Good Humor bars and Drumsticks are also part of Fred's childhood, although he is disdainful of the people who make Klondike Bars. He feels they've turned their backs on tradition by offering such travesties as almond, neapolitan, and cappuccino flavors. He wanted to substitute Eskimo Pies, but I felt there was something vaguely demeaning and anti-Inuit in the name. He settled for vanilla ice cream sandwiches because "If they're sandwiches, I can eat them for lunch, right?"

Fred likes Canadian bacon because it's round, tidy, and imported. He didn't, however, care for any of the strip bacon—until he saw a pack of lean turkey strips cunningly called Mr. Turkey. Nothing charms Fred like an animal, especially if it has an anthropomorphic name. I managed to use this to my advantage. Fred would ask if I thought we should get such-and-such item and I'd say, "I don't know, why don't you ask Mr. Turkey? Oh, that's right, you can't, he's dead." After doing this about three times, Fred scowled and said I'd spoiled it for him. He went back to the bacon section to return the late Mr. Turkey.

Returning from Mr. Turkey's final resting place, Fred discovered Oscar Mayer Lunchables. These are marvels of over-packaging offering six crackers, one-half ounce of sliced pressed meat, a cube of cheddar, a pouch of sugary juice, a tiny candy bar, and the notion that this could possibly be a balanced meal. He liked the concept, but this was all too much, even for him. In Frozen Foods, though, he found a brand called Kid Cuisine, which was similar to Lunchables except they made a stab at actual nourishment. You could choose their Cosmic Chicken Nuggets (For the New Age starchild on the go?), High-Flying Fried Chicken (And just how high can a dead, fried, frozen bird fly?), or Magical Macaroni & Cheese. That last one was not only magical but a wonder in monochrome, containing macaroni and cheese, corn, applesauce, and three lemon cookies. "Too yellow," declared Fred, knowing jewel tones suit him best. Another brand, Fran's Healthy Helpings, offered a meal-in-a-tray called Lucky Ducky Chicken with the chicken pressed into grim little duck shapes. I can't imagine that being seen in a positive light by either chickens or ducks. It's certainly not lucky for either. There was another meal from Fran called, I swear to God, Lovey Dovey Patty. It comes with heart-shaped pasta, a burger with a heart baked into the bun, and instructions on clotting because anyone seen eating this in a school yard will almost certainly get beaten up. How healthy is that, Fran?

In the deli section Fred found a package of vacuum-sealed miniature cheese balls. "They're like bon-bons!" he cried tossing them into the basket. "They're like a heart attack," I said, tossing them out. I don't know why I bother, though. The man can eat anything and it doesn't affect him. He eats Slim Jims by the yard. He will eat jerky from any land-based animal. I am certain he has ingested so many nitrites that if you sliced him, he'd look like prosciutto.

When we got it all home, it was amazing how little real food there was and how happy Fred was about it. He hummed merrily as he put cans of Cheez Whiz in the cabinet and fistfuls of turkey Gobble Stix in the fridge. "You know, I think I'll have some Eggos!" he said, beaming. "Want some?"

I remained distant and aloof. Call me old-fashioned, but I don't think waffles should be prepared vertically. That's OK, though. He has his food, and I have mine. I am the purist. I am the sensible one.

I am eating a Moon Pie.

"Hey, Fred," I ask, mouth full of marshmallow and cake, "where'd you put that frosting?"

TURKEY, HAM, AND OTHER DISASTERS

Ever wonder why we say Thanksgiving "rolls around"? It's because by the time it's passed we've eaten so much food that all we can do is roll around. When I was growing up in North Carolina, the holidays meant candied yams baked in butter and brown sugar, collards with fatback, green beans cooked with slabs of bacon, biscuits with thick gravy made from pan drippings and fat, and mashed potatoes running with rivers of melted butter. It's a wonder the South hasn't had a collective coronary. So how did something as healthy as turkey ever make it to the table? The answer is, it didn't. We had ham. Juicy, fatty, high-sodium, heart-clotting ham, and I couldn't get enough of it. If only for the love of ham, I could never be Jewish. I can live without my foreskin, but I gotta have my ham. I love ham so much I want to go like Mama Cass.

I discovered turkey only after I left the South. Delicious bird, it was nearly the national emblem thanks to Benjamin Franklin (who, ironically, was shaped rather like a ham). But it's the eagle that appears on the national emblem and the turkey that appears in the plastic Butterball casing. I say blessed be. And I do love the little plastic thingie that pops out indicating it's done so you don't discover your bird is undercooked while carving in front of four other couples, forcing you to hack it up and microwave it in gruesome chunks. Why, *why* didn't I cook a ham? The thing I was most thankful for that Thanksgiving was Jim Beam.

It was not my first turkey-related disaster. One

Thanksgiving our cousins sent us a turkey. It didn't replace our hallowed ham; it was merely granted temporary status as an exotic side dish. My father was wrestling a drumstick off the alien carcass for my little brother to eat on the floor. It wasn't punishment; my brother just liked eating off a plate by the cat dish—don't ask. Anyway, my father knocked a lit candle into the dried centerpiece, and suddenly we were all four dancing around the table beating at the flames until my mother dumped gravy on it. The laminate tabletop was singed and rippled, the tablecloth was ruined, the ceiling was black, and for weeks the house smelled of burned flowers and giblets.

In 1965 my father got my mother one of the first electric knives. We were visiting our cousins, who had cooked turkey, and Dad insisted she use it to carve. It didn't go well. With the flick of a switch the knife viciously chewed completely through the bird, cracked the platter, dug a six-inch gouge down a formal dining table, and sent three generations running for cover in the den. Years later when I saw *The Texas Chainsaw Massacre,* I remember thinking, "I've seen this before."

Although not strictly a disaster, there was also the time I ordered a turkey from HoneyBaked. I showed up to get it with my reservation number in hand only to be told mine had been sold. "*What?*" I was having a party that evening, and they were looking at a man who needed a turkey *now.* I pointed to the one cooked turkey I saw sitting behind the glass. "Nope," the manager said, "that's for somebody else— sorry." You do not tell a gay men expecting 20 people in two hours "sorry." I jumped the counter, grabbed the turkey, and even though I slapped $50 down by the register, I ran out feeling furtive yet exhilarated, like Dana Plato knocking over a video store. I remember thinking on the way home that I never had this kind of trouble with ham.

Whether turkey or ham, by nightfall I've eaten far too much of it and everything else. The belt is off, the pants are open, it isn't pretty. I've eaten so much it hurts, and thoughts cross my mind like, "Kate Moss does it three times a day; don't be such a wimp. Purge." But I don't because it's too much effort to get up and go down the hall. So I stay sprawled on the sofa, obsessing about a lifetime of overeating.

When it comes to food I have more issues than *Newsweek*. As a current Weight Watchers Lifetime Member (yes, above goal, and thank you for asking) I know how difficult food choices can be at the holidays. Two thin celery sticks or a slab of pecan pie? Soda water with lime wedge or eggnog with booze? I say forget the diet between Thanksgiving and New Year's and buy your holiday outfits with an eye to oversize sweaters and vertical stripes. Give yourself over to food, festivity, and friends in creative ways. Invite people over to decorate holiday cookies. I guarantee two things if you do: One, your cookies will look *fabulous,* and two, only a homosexual knows what dragées are so you can play Spot the Breeder! Just say, "Ted, could you pass me the dragées?" and if he doesn't hand you a tube of those edible little silver balls, you know he had trouble sitting through *Yentl.* Another festive fun food thing is to organize a traveling dinner. You get to eat all night, see everyone's home, and rifle through more medicine cabinets than the entire rest of the year. Last time we did that we served both ham and turkey and managed to avoid incident—if you don't count coming in to find the cats on the ham. "Quick, just turn it over while everyone's coming up the stairs! Who's gonna know!" Whatever you do, celebrate the season in all its disaster-prone caloric glory. Let the good times waddle.

If, like me, you visit your family over the holidays, you know what a comfort it can be to have a private stash of Häagen-Dazs and/or Stoli to take the edge off. How many times, as I've been carving the ham, have I been asked, "So, are you still seeing Fred?" Thus far I've resisted the urge to sling the electric carving knife across the table and shout

"No! I don't see him because when he's doing me I'm usually facedown!" Remember, as trying as they may be, your family needs gay little you in their lives. After all, what would the holidays be without at least one fruitcake?

WHAT KIND OF SICK PUPPY ARE YOU?

Playwright Edward Albee said, "We are all entitled to our perversions." Now, before the PC police take offense at the word *perversion,* let me just say that when it comes to my own predilections, I want them perverse, thank you. I want them damned perverse. Hell, that's the fun. Don't tell me they're normal explorations of sexuality; I want what I'm doing to give Jerry Falwell a coronary. (Now, *that* would be a rush.) But what about you? Who knows what "evil" lurks in your heart? Maybe there's something wonderful out there you haven't tried. The following test is designed to help you figure out your kinks. Into what delightfully dark corner does your mind naturally tend? You can also give this quiz to a partner to find out where his mind goes. Don't be squeamish, be experimental. Open yourself up, darling. And I'm not just talking about your legs.

That hunky guy at the gym left his jockstrap, which you know he hasn't washed in over a month, on the bench. You:
(a) Pick it up with a stick and drop it in the trash.
(b) Pick it up and take it home in your gym bag.
(c) Pick it up and wear it home on your face.

You want friends who will:
(a) Remember your birthday.
(b) Remember your birthday and come see you.
(c) Remember your birthday and come *on* you.

When you think of "cheese," you think of:
(a) A nice brie.
(b) Joan Collins.
(c) Foreskin.

Your date says he'd like to fist you. You inform him you will need:
(a) A cab home, *now.*
(b) A lot of patience, coaxing, poppers, and lube.
(c) Dinner and a movie first, thank you.

When someone says "pain," you think of:
(a) The time you rented *Spice World.*
(b) That burning sensation after your last trick.
(c) A good time, and then you cross your legs to hide that chubby you're getting.

When you think of "latex," you think of:
(a) Paint.
(b) Condoms.
(c) A complete party outfit with accessories.

Wearing women's clothing is:
(a) Silly.
(b) Only for drag queens.
(c) Damned expensive, but boy, is it worth it for the shoes!

Having sex with a transvestite is:
(a) Not your cup of tea.
(b) Only for celebrities.
(c) How you learned to accessorize.

When you shave, it is important to remember:
(a) How easy it is to nick your chin.

(b) Back hair grows back.

(c) Not to spray with Cruex for a day or two.

Having a wild three-way is:

(a) Not the sort of thing you could discuss with your partner.

(b) Not the sort of thing your partner would be willing to explore.

(c) Not the sort of thing your partner need ever find out about.

Your partner is uncomfortable watching you masturbate. You feel he:

(a) Needs more time to deal with intimacy issues.

(b) Ought to get in touch with his own feelings about self-gratification.

(c) Shouldn't have sat next to you on the bus in the first place.

Uniforms make you:

(a) Recall that hideous polyester number they made you wear at McDonald's.

(b) Think of our country's absurd "don't ask, don't tell" policy.

(c) Hard. Sir.

Leather is for:

(a) Cows.

(b) Shoes.

(c) 24/7.

Sadomasochism is:

(a) What you feel you've put up with all your life from your family.

(b) For people open to exploring pain and dominance as a door to sexual fulfillment.

(c) Only for perverts, baby, sick and twisted perverts. Believe it. Love it. Live it.

Bondage and discipline is:
(a) Wrong.
(b) Highly recommended for screaming kids in restaurants.
(c) $75 an hour. Plus tip.

Punishment and abuse are for:
(a) No one; there is no excuse for that in today's society.
(b) Holidays with your parents.
(c) *You,* you disgusting, vile, excremental excuse for a worm! Now get down on your knees and lick my filthy boots and *maybe* I'll let you bury your face in my stinking armpit!

You like to recycle:
(a) Cans and bottles because you can get cash for them.
(b) Because it's good for the environment.
(c) Beer.

"Scat" is:
(a) What you say to the kitty to get her off the bed.
(b) A classic form of blues singing.
(c) A good time Saturday night. And why you had corn for lunch.

If you said (c) to any of the above, you are ready to get into that particular fetish. If it's your first time, find someone to guide you, and enjoy. If you're already into it and it's someone else's first time, charge $100 an hour and tell them that's customary. (Hey, if it's their first time, how are they gonna know any different?)

If you said only (a) to all of the above, you are either more uptight than Jesse Helms at a K-Y convention or as clueless as my first lover, who thought "Greek active" meant making your own baklava. You need to get out there and experience things, my dear, so go. Just make sure you have a condom. And all your shots.

If you said (b) to most of the above, you're longing deeply to explore delectably perverse taboos but just can't bring yourself to take that final, fearsome step from which you may never return; you're acting all prim and proper, but underneath there's a seething desire for dark, decadent experience. Oh, god, the anguish! S'OK. You're the kind we (c) answerers love to get our hands on and ravish. Mainly because when your cherry gets popped, you're so ready they hear about it in the next county. Go on down to the bus station and wait. One of us perverts will be by directly.

And finally, if you're all concerned that this quiz (or any quiz in this book) doesn't score exactly like the others, get over it. What are you, some kind of sick freak?

PART SIX
Just Plain Ol' Being Gay

THE WORK OF BEING A GAY MALE

The demands of being a gay man are enormous. If I'd had any idea, I would have ditched that Barbie doll when I was five and learned how to throw a ball. I try to do my part to be a good queer, but it's utterly exhausting. Let me give a few examples.

First off, we have to know every Broadway musical ever produced and over 80 years of cinema. All of it. All the camp movies, the stars, the directors, everything. What straight boy is expected to know who did the choreography for Ross Hunter's *Lost Horizon,* music by Burt Bacharach, lyrics by Hal David? And if you don't know it was Hermes Pan, my guess is you're wearing something from the Hunt Club and you eat at Coco's. Oh, and who wrote the screenplay? Anyone? Anyone? Our own Larry Kramer, thank you. Don't know who that is? Try the buffalo wings.

We're expected to know all the latest glamour gossip as well as who's gay in Hollywood. How should I know who's gay in Hollywood? Hell, I can't tell who's gay in the grocery. But I must keep up appearances, so when I'm asked, "Is so-and-so gay?" I always say yes. I like to give everyone the benefit of the doubt.

Gay men are supposed to be terrific dancers. I suck. I'm also a lousy dancer. I don't merely move to the beat of a different drummer but of several competing drummers. Compared to other gays in dance clubs, I am the tragedy in the corner. The last time I was out at a club, somebody saw me dancing and called the paramedics. It wasn't pretty.

Speaking of pretty, it is mandatory we be highly looks-oriented. Therefore, I should be slaving away on some Exercycle at the gym. I tried it but it wasn't for me. Why would I want to go to a gym and pedal like mad only to go nowhere? I do that at work. I know some guys like muscle men, but when it comes to choosing a date my criteria do not include "capable of mindless, repetitive motion." For me, there was nothing interesting at the gym until I went into the steam room. Nice, but I can do that at a bathhouse without having to exercise first.

Which brings up the next item: As a gay man I am supposed to think of nothing but sex. Sex, sex, sex, 24 hours a day. I find this stereotype truly offensive. It has nothing to do with being gay. It has to do with being a *man.*

I'm also supposed to be skinny as a rail because thin is hot. Maybe for some, but not for me. I have a friend who watches *Trainspotting* the way I watch *Heatstroke*—and if you don't know what kind of a movie *Heatstroke* is, just know that Hermes Pan did not do the choreography (but I think he'd approve). I have dieted and dieted, and the only thing that looks better are liposuction ads. Lately, though, I am learning to accept my body for what it is and think positively: I am not overweight, I am well-marbled.

I'm expected to be obsessed with a man's "size," and you know I'm not talking about weight here. I'd like to care about size, but other, more important things get in my way, like "Can he construct a sentence?" and "He's not a Republican, is he?" For me, the hottest things a man can have are eye contact and a smile. You wanna talk size, show me a paycheck.

For some reason gay men are generally expected to not associate with lesbians, which I don't understand. I *love* my lesbian friends. "Hello, Rita, can you come over? That awful spider's back." Once, the oil light on my car lit up; I thought I'd won something. It took Linda to explain it to me *and* change the oil. Lesbians are the big sisters we all wished for when we were getting beaten up for wanting to play jump rope. As far as I'm concerned, lesbians are the best thing since Bette, Barbra, and Liza.

As a gay man I am expected to dress well and give comments about fashion on demand. Sometimes even without demand. I'm not very good at style stuff. The bright side of this is that since most anyone can tell I'm gay, people automatically assume I know fashion, and within a week they're wearing what I had on. Sometimes, though, I get irritated when a woman shopping for her husband asks me if this checkered tie goes with this striped shirt. I am tempted to say, "Why, yes!" because her husband isn't going to know, and until more people at work come out, nobody there is going to tell him. But I don't do that. I cut them some slack because they are women and in my book that makes them almost lesbians.

At the drop of a hat I'm supposed to be able to arrange flowers, furniture and formal brunches. I must hate sports, love opera, and cry when Judy Garland sings. But I can't and/or don't. What's wrong with me?

Since I'm not meeting expectations, could it be I'm not gay after all? Could it be time to call Dad and brighten his day? No, I can't give up sex with men. My lover, for one, would be very cranky. I'll stay queer for his sake and for the sake of our children, Mittens and Puff. But since it's too much work to live up to the demands of being a stereotype, I'll have to just be myself. Besides, people are much more interesting when they don't fit molds—or 28-inch waist pants, for that matter. I advise celebrating diversity, starting with yourself. I'm celebrating tonight with pizza, Diet Coke, fuzzy slippers, and *Hot Bear Daddies 5*. What's at your place?

MY ROSE-COLORED GOGGLES

What's all this hoopla over gays in the media? As far as I'm concerned gays have always been all over the media. Every day, everywhere I look, I see us in commercials, advertisements, billboards, brochures, and catalogs. How do I do it? Simple—I have Gay Goggles. Here's how they work.

You know that TV ad where Guy 1 wants to take Guy 2 to a ball game but Guy 2 can't go because he has all this stuff to do, including looking up dinosaurs for his son's report, and Guy 1 shows him he can do it all online? Put on the patented Gay Goggles *et voilà*, they're a queer couple raising Guy 2's son together. As another example, take that commercial that purports to show an older father giving sage financial advice to his grown son. In my world it's a Daddy/Boy relationship and the K-Y is in the drawer next to the tit clamps. When these two go out, the younger one has a chain with a padlock around his neck and Daddy holds a leash. Not bad for a 30-second spot, huh? You'd be amazed how far I can get in an ad that runs a full minute. This wonderful perspective is all due to my Gay Goggles. They take the straight world and translate it to suit me.

I developed the Goggles when I was about 13. I was flipping through the Sears catalog while eating an entire one-pound package of Chips Ahoy in my bedroom when it hit me. How else could one look at all these athletic men chumming around in their underwear? My adolescent imagination invented conversations between them like, "Wanna come over to my parents' garage and help me work on my bike?" "Will you be wearing that all-cotton Munsingwear brief?" "No, at home I wear the Fruit of the Loom classic boxer because I like how it gaps when I sit." "Keen! I'll wear the fitted Jantzen swim trunks featured on page 259." Yes, these were the very same men who, mere pages later, were gathered poolside smiling at something—or someone—just off-camera. I'd angle the page so I could imagine they were looking at me. "Hi, guys," I'd say. "Why, hello, Joel," the lanky one I'd named Rocko would answer, "you're looking spiffy in your Hawaiian-inspired print baggies, but why don't you take off that matching terry cloth beach jacket?" "Uh, no, that's OK," I'd murmur. "Forget about it," Rocko would say with a warm smile, "we were gonna head over to page 438 anyway and stand around in khakis and polo knits. Wanna come?" "Gee, could I, Rocko?" "Of course, Joel. Many are available in husky sizes."

I realize there's a fine line between having an active imagination and being delusional, but when you believe you're the only person in the world who has these feelings, you get lonely, you get desperate, and you get creative. It was survival. It was also fun. And I was off and running.

I next used my youthful Goggles on *Adam 12,* where Pete Malloy and Jim Reed were squad car partners. They were about as stiff and wooden as the Sears models, but they were cops so the whole uniform thing came into play. They spent all day cruising back streets and alleys in L.A.'s Rampart District, which I grew up to learn included the very gay neighborhood of Silver Lake. Hmm! On *Emergency* there were yummy paramedics John Gage and Roy DeSoto. "C'mon, Roy, let's *roll!*" Later it was A.J. and Rick on *Simon & Simon* with the added taboo that they were brothers. On *CHiPS* Ponch and John had tight uniforms *and* motorcycles. *Starsky and Hutch* had leather jackets that kept me up at night. I had a field day with *The Streets of San Francisco* because, well, it was San Francisco. More recently there was *My Two Dads,* featuring Michael and Joey, two guys so stupid they didn't know which one had impregnated Nicole's mom. I figured if they were that clueless about breeding, my making them gay was doing the world a favor.

My Goggles showed me that pairings between dominant and submissive men were a norm. How else could you explain why mysterious but wealthy Robin Masters allowed Magnum P.I. to live on his estate and drive his expensive, sporty car all over the island solving mysteries and attracting rough trade? Gilligan and the Skipper slept together in their hut (and who'd have figured Gilligan as the top?). As for kinky, four words: Mr. Roarke and Tattoo. "Smiles, everybody!"

Gay Goggles aren't just for television either. Those hunky cowboys on the cigarette billboards got mighty lonesome in my world. As they got more horny and less picky, I saw them lighting more than each other's smokes—and I got all that out of a lousy print ad while waiting for the light to change.

In music there's that Garth Brooks album where he looks like he's got friends not only in low places but back rooms, too. He's standing there as if he's been invited to a private party and could use a ride. And then there's Brooks and Dunn, two men who wear fabulous shirts and sing country duets to each other. With these guys, who needs Goggles?

Along those lines, how about Siegfried and Roy? These two are already so "out there" that I'm forced to go beyond the obvious and imagine they're actually post-operative transsexual lesbians. What else would explain all those cats?

Television, though, is still where I use my Goggles most. I especially enjoy them while watching *American Gladiators,* pro wrestling, and after-game locker room interviews. Other prime candidates are military movies, westerns and anything involving pirates. Hell, I've gotten so adept at this, I can watch C-SPAN and matchmake senators—which I think might be a good place to stop. Pairing up right-wingers may be wicked fun, but it sure isn't pretty.

We all know that most people on TV are not gay. Not even the gay ones, which is really annoying. For those out there striving to change that, you have my personal gratitude, applause, and support. Just the same, though, I'm going to keep my Gay Goggles. After all, some people choose to see things the way they are and ask "Why?" while others choose to see what ought to be and ask "Why not?" I, however, choose to see what amuses me and say "Girlfriend!"

LE FREAK, C'EST CHIC

If you need to know if you're in style, ask a gay man and he will tell you. Actually, he will probably tell you without your asking. He'll also tell your friends, family, and anybody else who will listen. This isn't bitchiness; this is our gift. So with your indulgence, I'd like to bitch—I mean share my gift—about some of the current trends.

I notice the fashion in automobiles, at least in L.A., seems to be behemoth cars each carrying exactly one person. These tanks are impossible to see around, and the only thing you can do to keep a level playing field is buy one yourself, thereby becoming an irritant to other normal-size cars. Why does anyone need 200 feet of cargo space when the most they're carrying around is a fragile ego, condoms, and a toothbrush? Can you say "making up for deficiencies in other areas"? Whatever sad psychological condition these people are carrying in all that space is a windfall for the oil companies because these great lumbering beasts only get 20 feet to the gallon. In the long run, therapy would be cheaper.

If driving the Ford Brontosaurus is "in," I notice using one's turn signals is decidedly "out," regardless of model. Accident lawyers are probably behind that. Also "out" is the use of car ashtrays. Every day I see people flicking their still-burning cigarette butts out the window, no doubt proud of the fact California leads the nation in brushfires. The ability to control one's car alarm is apparently another "out." People who have to futz frantically with their car alarms for ten min-

utes every time they park or start their cars are proclaiming
to the world, loudly and obnoxiously, just how stupid they
are. But hey, they're cool, right? Yeah.

It's easy enough to keep up with the new hairstyles. If you
try one and it looks stupid, you can always recut it or leave
town while it grows back out. If you can't go somewhere nice
like San Francisco, go to Bakersfield, where it doesn't seem to
matter what you look like. The current hair trend for men
was obviously the brainchild of the people who make mousse
and gel. It's two inches of hair going straight up, then abrupt-
ly banking to one side. The only other option is the sexy rat's
nest. At first glance it looks like the person ran into a hedge
trimmer, but there's all the difference in the world between
the guy who dropped $125 for it and the schmo who got it at
Supercuts. And we can tell too. It's the difference between a
Jackson Pollock and spilled paint. I don't have the money,
patience, or amount of hair to do much of anything, plus I got
tired of all the gray, so I just shaved what I had left. Took me
all of two minutes. Unfortunately, it's beginning to look like I
may have to do that with my chest and shoulders too, and
that's gonna take mu-u-uch longer.

The style for the leather community tends toward the traditional—straps, harnesses, buttless chaps—which is good
because for what this stuff costs it would be impossible to
keep up with a changing style. I have noticed the occasional
kilt or Roman centurion–style skirt, but I don't think that's so
much about fashion as ease of access. One night I made an
unintentional leather fashion statement myself. In my hurry I
grabbed not my black leather cap but a black cloth cap. I
threw it on figuring the bar's dark, so what would it matter?
All night long it seemed I met only musical theater leather
queens. I wondered why that was until I got home and I realized my manly, butch black cap had FOSSE stitched across it in
glaring white. At least I was able to actually talk to people.
I'm thinking about wearing my JACQUES BREL hat next time

and seeing if I can meet *un homme cuir français.* (Note to self: Find a French safeword I can pronounce under duress.)

I'm not particularly into tattoos, although I have come to respect them. Fred has several including tribalistic lizards, blue dolphins, and *The Partridge Family* logo. I've thought about getting one, but the fact that they are so in style now gives me pause because the hottest thing today can become a joke in no time. I have college photos of me in a paisley shirt with fringe and a shoulder-wide collar. I can burn the shirt and even the photos, but with a tattoo I'd be stuck (no pun intended). Instead, I had my nipples pierced, which, should fashions change, can heal over, giving me plausible deniability.

If you are considering getting your nips pierced, let me give you a word of warning. Everybody says, "It doesn't hurt." They lie. It's surgical steel going through sensitive flesh; you do the math. I had it done at the L.A. pride festival in a booth near the parking structure. I stood in line behind three lesbians who got their tongues and lips pierced with nary a sound. When I got it in the nipple, I let out a yell that set off a nearby car alarm. I think it was one of those stupid Dodge Mega-Mammoths, and it took the owner a full 15 minutes of futzing to turn it off. No surprise there. Anyway, as soon as the pain from the initial piercing was over, it was OK. Now that they've healed, I love 'em. When I showed Fred, though, he scoffed, saying, "What are you going to do with those when you go visit your parents at Christmas?" I was considering red ribbons and mistletoe.

So much for the trends as they are now. There are some styles I'm in favor of starting. For instance, we need fewer dot-coms and more dot-orgs. People need to go to the library at least as often as they go to the gym. Churches need to get out of the hate business and get their minds around this "God is love" idea. Lawmakers need to get into depressed economic regions and out of my ass. And will someone please tell

Madonna to knock it off with that British accent; she's from Michigan, for crying out loud.

There are some things we could do with less of, including places serving $3 coffee, parking enforcement nazis, Frank Wildhorn musicals, hate served up as love, anything with Adam Sandler, machines that call and tell you to "please hold for an important message," and people who don't know that when the movie starts they're supposed to *shut the fuck up,* thank you.

Here are some things we could do with a lot more of: free samples of ice cream and cake, tolerance on all fronts (unless they're talking in the movies), whimsy in the workplace, glamour on the big screen, nearly naked men in advertising, and simple common courtesy everywhere. I like to think that with enough courtesy we'd get the tolerance, but I'm really big on the ice cream and cake thing.

But what about queer people? I was concerned when we first started hearing about "lesbian and gay chic" a couple of years ago. I remember a coworker telling me, "You're lucky you're gay. It's so fashionable now." Usually when you're "in" things go your way. You get privileges, rights, that kind of thing. So my question is, "When were we in?" I must have missed that day because I don't remember getting squat.

I don't think I want to be fashionable anyway. Sure, it may be fun while we're in vogue, but being in vogue can go south faster than, well, vogueing. What's left then? We have to hang out for 15 years until we become retro? No, thanks.

Oh, but what am I worried about? We are beyond the whims of fashion. Since the first Cro-Magnon queer made his older sister an animal skin wrap with a smart leather tie above the waist, cap sleeves, and a scoop neck, we have been dictating the fashion for everyone else. So, look out world— piss us off by calling us "unfashionable" and we'll bring back bell-bottoms.

Hmm. Maybe that's what happened.

POP QUIZ—How "Martha" Are You?

Martha Stewart has turned us all into home and hearth experts. Or has she? Phenomenally successful as she is, there are still those among us who think flower-patterned drapes with deedly-ball fringe are chic. I actually knew one man so nondomestic he thought deedly-balls were what his first lover had. At any rate, it's time we faced the fact some of us are faking it, and not just in the bedroom. Do you have a Cordon Bleu certificate in French cuisine, or do you have Domino's on speed-dial? Do you have the interior design touch or are you papering your rumpus-room with pictures from the Steve Kelso Shrine Page on the Internet? Are you more apt to be found navigating an English garden or cruising the park? Take the following test and find out where you fall on the house-culture continuum:

Copper verdigris is:
(a) A charming patina on weathered copper.
(b) Your drag name.
(c) That fungus you caught at the baths.

A pineapple finial is:
(a) A pineapple-shaped feature to decorate the bottom of your banister.
(b) A devious dessert to destroy any diet.
(c) Pineapple juice, grenadine, and enough rum to make your date look better.

A "200 count" describes your:
(a) Egyptian cotton bed linens.
(b) Goal number of sit-ups.
(c) Bedroom traffic since June.

A fine crackle finish can be found on:
(a) Your early American antique furniture.
(b) Your bedsheets.
(c) Your slutty ex's chin.

Forcing a bulb is:
(a) Done in the late winter for early spring blooms.
(b) A sure way to get electrocuted.
(c) A euphemism for time in the bathroom after eating too much cheese.

You discover ramekins in your kitchen. You consider:
(a) Making individual country-baked fruit tartlets.
(b) Chasing them the hell out with a broomstick and then calling their parents.
(c) Professional fumigation.

Composting is:
(a) The environmentally sound way to provide fertilizer for your vegetable garden.
(b) For people who can't afford regular trash collection.
(c) What you did to your boyfriend's personal papers, photos, tax receipts, stock certificates, savings bonds, clothes, and CD collection after you caught him with the cable guy.

You are disappointed with your figworts. Next time you will:
(a) Plant in a rich, slightly alkaline soil.
(b) Have some Compound W handy.
(c) Insist on a condom.

Your boyfriend gives you pergolas. This means:

(a) You have lovely arched trellises you can place over a path or walkway.

(b) You're gonna itch like crazy until you get rid of them.

(c) A trip to the clinic. Again.

If you were to encounter a hand dibbler, you might consider:

(a) Planting fringed starburst iris bulbs with it.

(b) A manicure, because it's been ages since you had your hands dibbled.

(c) Joining him, hoping you don't get caught dibbling there in the steam room at Bally's.

SCORING: Give yourself ten points for each (a) answer, five points for each (b) answer and 1 point for each time you answered (c).

100 to 70 points: You are *so-o-o* gay! You could whip up french and goblet pleated pelmets in your sleep while the rest of us are trying to figure out what the hell pelmets are and living with bare miniblinds. You are a man who would have your nipples pierced just so you could hang silk tassels. Other men come to you when they want you to glaze their *croquembouche,* and I'm not talking metaphorically. You could teach Martha a thing or two, so you go, girl, and charge the rest of the world an arm and a leg for it.

69 to 21 points: You have just enough homemaking savvy to know your place looks like hell but not enough to know what to do about it. You suspect a tieback is not a football position, but you're not sure. You are uncomfortable around an occasional table because if it's only occasionally a table, it may occasionally be something else, and you don't like surprises. You are not alone. Many of us are not homemaking do-it-yourselfers, but fortunately we can always order in. For your next affair—and no, I'm not talking about what you're doing with the gardener—call a good caterer, and no one will

be the wiser. Remember, in a service economy one can always rent class.

20 points or below: Oh dear, oh dear. You are why God made Wal-Mart. You wouldn't know a Biedermeier torchère if it bit you in the aspic. You think Chenille is a character on *Moesha*. If someone said you had terra-cotta pot feet, you'd punch their lights out. You're so butch, you're practically a lesbian. As Martha would say, though, that's a good thing. The world needs gay good ol' boys. God knows I do.

So, did you find yourself in one category and your boyfriend in another? Not to worry, and I speak from experience. Homemaking is fine but give me someone who knows how to wreck a room and leave rug burns and I can live without the stenciled wood floors, the carpaccio on French bread, and the ruched swags and tails. I used to despair when my honey would hang Disney movie posters next to my museum art prints. I've come to learn it doesn't matter if all his taste is in his mouth as long as I'm in there, too. Remember, home is where the hard is. Er, heart. Right.

LET'S NOT GET PHYSICAL

Everybody wants to look good. That's why Avon goes door-to-door, Bally's 24 Hour Fitness gyms stay open all night, and I should own stock in Clinique. These days, however, my Avon lady is selling Herbalife, the Clinique is working less and less, and my work wardrobe consists entirely of slimming blacks and bold vertical stripes. Depending on the day, I look like an East Village nihilist or a barbershop tenor. Clearly, it's time for me to hit the gym.

I do not look forward to this. The last time I joined a gym it was because I wanted to watch men undress and have access to a Jacuzzi. Once I discovered the baths, step aerobics lost its appeal. But Fred and I have agreed to suspend those visits so it's back to the dumbbells, not to mention the free weights they use.

OK, I'm being grossly unfair. There are plenty of intelligent people at the gym. There exist gay Republicans too, and when I meet them I'm always just as surprised. I have to admit I'm being catty only because I'm terribly intimidated by obviously superior physical specimens. The whole place is full of people already ripped. Where's the gym you go to to get in good enough shape to go to a gym? I never see anyone pudgy like me and it makes me nervous. I fear that at some hidden signal all these unnaturally beautiful people are going to surround me and stuff me into some holding pit for the unsightly and flabby. It'll have one-way mirrors so we can be pointed at by Thor and Inga as bad examples. "If you don't work out 12 hours a day, you'll look like him." "Ew! The hairy one shaped like mashed potatoes?" "Ja!"

One reason I don't like these places is the staff can be so rude. Once I asked for another towel, and they told me to go back to the locker room and put on a shirt and some shorts. Nobody tells you workout etiquette either. I don't know how to claim dibs on a machine. I laid a quarter on the StairMaster, and it didn't seem to mean a thing to anyone. And I lost my quarter. Another time I called and called for a spotter and was ignored. Of course, I was in the shower at the time. And did you know if you change the channel during a ball game to something interesting like, say, *From Martha's Kitchen,* everybody gets all bent out of shape?

Speaking of television, how on earth can someone watch the evening news while running on a treadmill? I can't respond to this week's firing of the Russian cabinet when I'm busy sucking oxygen and wheezing. If I'm going to watch something, it needs to be motivating, uplifting, and dirty. Give me New World Video's *Link 2 Link* starring Corey Jay and see if I don't run toward that. Just remind me to wear a dance belt that day.

I also loathe aerobics. You go into a room with two dozen people who can legitimately wear spandex (I *hate* that). They're all impossibly perky, jumping up and down to double-time disco, multiplied into gleeful legions from Day-Glo hell by four walls of mirrors. After blacking out one time, I had the out-of-body experience of seeing myself in the mirror across the room surrounded by perfect people asking the fat sweaty guy sprawled on the floor if they should call 911. I lay there looking up the shorts of Lars, the massive aerobics leader. He wasn't all that buffed, but what I was seeing was indeed massive. Suddenly a young woman leaned into view.

"Can I do anything?"

"Move."

"He wants to be moved!" she shouted, and a dozen well-chalked hands hoisted me upright so I could again experience the spinning stars and colors. I staggered out in hallucinatory shame vowing never to return.

Several months ago a friend told me if I didn't want to go to a gym, I should get active through sports, so I tried that. I took up Putt-Putt, Foosball, and canasta. No weight came off, and they serve food with canasta. Useless.

I even looked into this month's hot new thing: a spinning class. That's where you pay money to be told how to ride a stationary bike. It's done in massive groups, and you're supposed to get encouragement from the others as they shout out things like "Come on!" and "Keep going!" and "You can do it!" over the difficult parts. That was all just too annoying for me. I was shouting out things like "You're all a bunch of fascists!" and "Fuck you!" and "I'm having a coronary!" I was not invited back.

Screw 'em. They didn't have a Jacuzzi, anyway.

Even if I did join a damn gym, the question remains, which one? For a while Fred belonged to a gym that, although convenient, was expensive in order to "keep out the riffraff." Hell, that's exactly the kind of people I was paying a premium to meet elsewhere.

Upon further reflection, I think it is shallow of me to be so concerned with the external. I see now that the answer lies elsewhere. I don't need to start going to a gym; I need to start going to bear bars. They know how to appreciate us full-figure gals. Besides, I kinda likes 'em on the burly side. Oh, sure, I expect my porno to be slick and perfect, but I also expect it back in the drawer inside of three minutes. I want a real man who looks like a real man, extra poundage and all. So forget the pain and rigors of the gym, and bring on the hefty lumberjacks.

Woof!

SPORTS

I admit it. I had to do some research for this one. Not that I minded. It was nice to have a legitimate excuse for hanging out in locker rooms. I even watched something called the Super Bowl. I loved it; the commercials were fabulous, and the winning team seemed genuinely enthusiastic about it. You go, boys! I went to tournaments, meets, and games like mad to see what this sports thing was all about. As nearly as I can tell, it's pretty much hitting or kicking things in a group and pulling at your gonads. This has been very educational for me. Before this I thought a biathlete was David Bowie on a treadmill. Heck, I thought pocket pool was a sport. I certainly played it like it was. Through my research, however, I learned otherwise, and I have come to appreciate athletes. Oh, and what they do in their sport, too. Now it's your turn to find out how much you know:

In a track and field relay race, what does one do with the baton?
(a) Pass it.
(b) Twirl it.
(c) Work it, girlfriend.

An excellent example of a men's voluntary floor exercise would be:
(a) A full-twisted double-back salto.
(b) Sit-ups to get rid of those love handles.

(c) Anything that leaves rug burns and a smile.

How many balls do you need to play eight-ball pool?
(a) Sixteen, including the cue ball.
(b) Eight. Huh, can't fool me.
(c) Two, duh. We're guys, hel-*lo*?

Greg Louganis is:
(a) A big queer Olympic gold medal–winning diver battling HIV, and we love him.
(b) Way too good for that bitch Steve Kmetko.
(c) Hot, but no Mario Lopez.

The choice of "ends" and the "right to serve" is determined by:
(a) A coin toss prior to table tennis.
(b) The referee you flirted with.
(c) Whomever pays for dinner.

If you know what "the bully" is in field hockey and that a softball is 11⅞ to 12⅛ inches around, you are:
(a) Qualified to call both games.
(b) Spending way too much time on trivial things, especially with Prince Edward in this sham of a marriage.
(c) A lesbian.

If you were near a T-bar, you would be:
(a) Skiing.
(b) Drinking.
(c) Cruising the T-bartender.

Mark McGwire and Sammy Sosa:
(a) Both beat Roger Maris's 1961 record for the most home runs in a season.
(b) Are copresidents of Black and White Men Together.

(c) Show their bats and balls in Chi Chi LaRue's classic *Double Play in the Dugout*.

Handballing requires:
(a) Two players, gloves, a ball, and a court.
(b) Two players, a porno theater, and very heavily buttered popcorn.
(c) Two players, patience, lube, and a sling.

The point of jai alai is:
(a) To hit the ball (*poleta*) with a wicker basket (*cesta*) against the front wall in such a way that your opponent can't return it.
(b) To make money (*moola*) by betting against the American (*white guy*).
(c) To meet (*shag*) sexy Cubans (*hunkoramas*).

If you are dribbling, you:
(a) Are playing basketball.
(b) Need to start paying attention to those June Allyson ads.
(c) Should have used a condom.

If you have just won the Stanley Cup, that means:
(a) You and your team are National Hockey League champions.
(b) You can wear it to protect your Stanley Jewels.
(c) You progress to the lightning round, where you could win the rest of your Stanley place setting and matching flatware.

Scoring: 5 points for every (a) answer, 3 points for each (b) answer, and 1 point per (c) answer.

60 to 50 points: You da man! Grunt and spit, you big sweaty receptacle of testosterone-trained trivia. You know

enough about rowing to forgo obvious comments regarding coxed pairs. You know that hurling is a game and not what happens when you mix peppermint schnapps and Ripple. You must be so proud. You can quote RBIs out the a-s-s, but I am here to tell you they are not the stats the rest of us are interested in. Nothing is more boring at the bar than hearing about your baseball fantasy team. Some of us have different fantasies, OK? So you know your sports; hooray for you. Go somewhere and procreate, why don't you.

49 to 30 points: You have an idea about sports but not enough to "pass" at the watercooler at work. You know your NFL from your NBA, but suspect paddleball involves S/M. You watch figure skating because you like anything where "sit and spin" is compulsory. On the other hand, you're angry with the IOC because they won't allow Rudy Galindo to skate pairs with Brian Boitano. Oops, I mean Brian Orser. The point is that just because you know that a three-day event involves horses and not your mother over Memorial Day does not mean you're ready to tailgate-party with breeders. They'll know you're an imposter when you show up with the arugula salad.

29 to 12 points. Oh, honey, go back to your *Martha Stewart Living*. You don't have a clue about sports. You think curling requires gel. You believe *The David Kopay Story* is a Broadway musical. When people talk of the California Angels you assume they mean Sabrina, Jill, and Kris. In your world, sudden death does not involve overtime but a sneer from Mr. Blackwell. The only sporting you do is a woody in the steam room. You're bat-blind, scared of the ball, gun-shy, and you run like a girl. You are so me! To hell with this jock stuff, girlfriend, let's do lunch and go shopping. Now *that's* my kind of sport.

HOW NOT TO WORK AT WORK

From the beginning of time man has had to work. While working, he pondered the question: "How the hell can I get out of doing this?" Well, kids, I'm going to tell you.

Know your facility. Where do people go? Where do they not go? Find out and go to the latter, not the former. Duh, right? You'd think, but there are people at my company who kill time in the coffee room. *Everyone* goes to the coffee room. For crying out loud, *go somewhere else*. When I worked at McDonald's and couldn't stand the thought of flipping another fatty burger, I'd put on a parka and hang in the walk-in freezer. I froze my ass off, but I wasn't working.

Look busy. Props are essential for this. Walking the halls is merely malingering unless you have a printout in hand or a broken tool or whatever works for you at your job. At Kerr Glass I hated being at my desk. My boss was the VP of Employee Relations, so, wouldn't you know, that damn phone just rang all day long. Worse, I had to answer with a rhyme: "Joel Perry, secretary." I had to get away, but with only a busy coffee room on-site, where could I hide? The answer was: in plain sight. I was seen huffing up and down hallways, dashing between departments, fidgeting while waiting for elevators, all with a bogus file folder and great intent of purpose. I had such a reputation for being busy that the other secretaries looked up in awe as I passed. The irony was that they were sitting at their desks working, watching me whiz by doing nothing.

If you don't like doing something, never do it well. I learned this early as a pimply-faced peon at McDonald's. I loathed unloading the truck and putting supplies away on the high shelves in the storeroom. So I tossed enormous 3-by-3-by-4 boxes of cup lids up there with such abandon that I knocked out the fluorescent lights in glorious showers of sparks and frosted shards. Three lights in 15 minutes, and I was returned to pouring drinks. Years later, as the only male secretary at Kerr Glass, my VP boss would occasionally forget and ask me to get him coffee. I resented this so much I mixed cigarette ashes in with his 1½ packs of Sweet'n Low, knowing it would buy me another six months before he got his taste buds back and asked me again. At my current job I write and produce radio comedy. You know, creative stuff. Last year my boss demanded I present him with graphs, invoices, budgets, spreadsheets, and other bean-counter crap. I learned just enough Lotus 1-2-3 to wreck the hard drive so thoroughly that our company gave up trying to fix it and switched to Excel. I have not been bothered with so much as a pie chart since.

Always overestimate how long it will take you to do an assignment. If you can do it in ten minutes, say it will take half an hour. Do it and get it over with in ten minutes, then call a friend and gossip for the next ten. When you hang up, *then* hand in your assignment. You've wasted fully as much time as you worked, and you've turned your work in ten minutes sooner than expected, *thereby impressing your boss.* Is this a beautiful world or what?

Never turn in a large assignment the moment you are done. Wait. Then wait some more. Remember, when you turn in work, they're only going to give you more. So just wait. You'll think of something to do with that time. Keep those papers or whatever spread on your work space, and don't hand them in until about 4:30. By then your boss will be so desperate for it that when you hand it over he'll be thrilled. Plus 4:30 is too late in the day to expect you do much else.

Just in case, though, go play out that remaining half hour in the bathroom. That's what it's for.

Take long lunches. Here's how: When your boss leaves for his hourlong lunch at 12, make sure he sees you slaving away. Wait until 12:10 to make sure he's really gone, then put a fake phone message on his desk that says something like "Barnaby called, will call back later—12:51." Your boss will return at 1, assume you spent from 12 to 12:51 working, and time your return from lunch from the bogus 12:51 message, giving you until almost 2. You just bought yourself an hour-and-45-minute lunch.

Never let them know what you know how to do. Can you fix the copier? Read DOS? Do calligraphy? Do it once, and you'll do it forever. No, no, no, my dears. Beg off snaking that toilet, or you will be the company plumber until you retire.

You are the expert, even when you're not. Whatever your job may be, you probably handle equipment you know intimately, often a computer, about which your boss is clueless. On this hateful equipment you will at some time be asked to do something complex, large, and what is really unforgivable, boring. Rehearse this phrase: "It can't be done." You're the expert. How is he gonna know otherwise? And even if he calls you on it, simply express surprise and say, "Wow, can you show me?" That way he ends up doing the work while you watch. Need I remind you, watching is not working? The best, though, is if he should say, "Oh, yeah? Well, Nancy does it all the time," because then you get to say, "Really? Goodness me. Then perhaps Nancy should do this too." If he doesn't look like he's buying it, simply add, "I'd hate to get it wrong and have it reflect poorly on you when you show it to the big boss." Just remember to bring brownies for Nancy because she will be doing your work.

Know when the cat's away. Better than that, know when the cat's *going to be* away. After all, you have a social life to plan for.

Never volunteer—*ever*—unless it takes you off premises. Who wants to rearrange the file room, organize the Secret Santa, be the Fire Safety Monitor? Not, repeat, not you. Especially with that orange vest they make monitors wear. But who wants to, say, take something to the warehouse, dash out for a birthday cake, pick up the boss's dry cleaning? You, honey, you! Once you're off premises your life is your own and simple errands expand to fill entire afternoons. While you're lounging with your double decaf mochaccino, birthday cake melting in the car, you have time to relax, do the crossword, get to know your *barista,* and ponder the important questions like, How did Oprah get in bed with Starbucks to sell books?

Never let the big boss learn your name. It will be the one name he remembers and calls on. If he stops you and asks your name, give him the name of the guy who tried to make you Fire Safety Monitor.

All work is the same. Your job, your doctor's, the pimply-faced peon's pulling Mr. Pibb at McDonald's, everyone's job is this: Getting rid of all the stuff that comes your way before even more stuff comes. I realized this when I had a job at Equitable Insurance that was so bleak I'm certain parts of the movie *Brazil* were filmed there. I would come in every morning to find my "In" basket full of stuff I had to take care of, eventually moving it to my "Out" basket by the end of the day. After about a month of this meaningless drudgery I realized that all I had to do was move everything in the "In" basket to the "Out" basket and life became a breeze. It couldn't be too obvious, though, so I developed a cunning plan. I'd spread everything from my "In" basket all over my desk, sprinkle it with pencils and paper clips and go out for coffee. I'd come back around 11:30, rearrange the mess on my desk, be seen, and then go to lunch. Lunch being a verb that included shopping, manicures, and, not infrequently, a movie. Around 4 I'd return to complain about the workload and kibitz with the other cogs. At 4:45 I'd stack the stuff on my desk, dump it in the "Out" basket, and hit the rest room until 5. Once during "lunch" I went to a fortune-teller who told me, "You are unhappy in your job." Gee, a man in a tie seeing a psychic at 3 in the afternoon, it doesn't take Jeane Dixon to figure that one.

Sometimes the workplace gets so oppressive, you just can't stand the thought of going in. You have no sick days left and using a precious vacation day is out of the question. You need a good excuse. Which brings us to another rule: If it's worth lying about, it's worth a damn good lie. When I was a breakfast waiter at a Holiday Inn in downtown Washington, D.C., we were told we could have our birthdays off. When mine came up, I asked for it and was summarily denied. I woke up on my birthday and decided there was no way in hell I was going in. I needed a lie, but I needed one so audacious that when I did go in I wouldn't get any flack about it. So I called them up and told them my roommate's mother had committed suicide. Not only that, but I needed to take him to Baltimore to identify her. The reaction over the phone was even better than anticipated, so I took the next two days off too. When I went back, the news had somehow gotten mangled such that they thought it was my mother who had died. I did not disabuse them of the notion. It was the only damn time they ever treated me with anything approaching consideration. Incidentally, if I ever served you, I apologize. As you may have guessed, my heart was not in breakfast waitering.

OK, that should give you plenty of impetus to start you wasting glorious amounts of time at your job. These are merely the basics, but they are tried-and-true and beautiful things indeed. Your life at work has just become easier. Unless you work for yourself. In that case you are screwed.

HOW MUCH TO YOU LOVE ME?

It's Valentine's Day! A day of tender transcendence commemorated by the ritual offering of a gift, given as a tiny token of the joy you and your loved one share in your united soul.

Yeah, right. We're that deep. The reality is we've bought into the media's message that $=♥, which makes us about as deep as a Dixie Cup. That's our damage, so let's deal with it. Valentine's Day means loving someone just ain't enough. You gotta go out and buy something to quantify that love. And oh, the pitfalls!

There's the double-blind second-guessing for starters. You have to estimate how much you think your mate loves you in terms of the dollars you think he will spend on you and then find a gift that is not only in the same price range but that you think he will enjoy. Overspend, and you make him look bad. Underspend, and you are a heartless skinflint and bastard. Either way, do not think that flowers the following day will make up for your error. That's what the rest of your life is for.

So how much do you spend? One gauge for knowing how far to go is to ask yourself what you would be willing to sacrifice for your boopsie-boo. A major limb? Then getting him a lavish bouquet will suffice. You're obviously in that just-met-and-still-haven't-fully-thought-this-through stage, so fluff will do just fine—this year. Are you willing to give up a vital organ? If so, you are in a more serious relationship, which, unfortunately, may require jewelry. Would you be willing to give up going to a party at, say, David Geffen's? If so, then you and your honey are ready to buy real estate.

There is also the question of what the gift you are giving says. Does that adorable stuffed animal you bought say "You are my cutesy-pootsy Pooh Bear of snuggly wuvvy-wuvvum" or "I'm dating chicken"? It goes both ways too. When the light of your life gave you that ten-pound box of Godiva chocolates, was he saying "Sweets for the sweet" or "I find your success with Jenny Craig a threat"? Because of the highly complex nature of relationships in general and Valentine's gift-giving in particular, I have provided below an annotated gift-giving Q&A to get you started.

Giving your sweetie gold cuff links says:
(a) I want you to know I love you.
(b) I want you to start dressing better.
(c) I want to lock your ass into an ironclad commitment, damn it.

If it is commitment you're after, it's best to start with something small, like giving him his own toothbrush for when he stays over. It may take days or even weeks to build up to choosing a china pattern, joint tenancy, insulting each other's friends, and substituting bickering for sex. Like the song says, you can't hurry love.

An out-of-town getaway says:
(a) I want to spend time with you.
(b) I want to go where nobody I know will see me with you.
(c) I want you to know you're so lousy in bed I need housekeeping and room service to put me over the top.

Going out of town is always a big risk. You are literally and figuratively on unfamiliar territory. Did you spend so much time finding the restaurant that the hunger took you from cranky to at-each-other's-throat? It's going to be a long, cold, grim trip back. Stay somewhere in town. And carry snacks in the car.

A dozen long-stemmed red roses says:
(a) I have no imagination.
(b) I have no imagination.
(c) I have no imagination.

If this is all you can come up with for a Valentine gift, how imaginative can you be in the sack? You might as well wear a sign that says BAD LAY. Of course, given the number of those I hear about from my friends, this could be why there are so many florists.

The gift of cologne says:
(a) I'm tired of you smelling like an ox.
(b) I'm tired of you smelling like my ex.
(c) I'm tired of you smelling like your ex.

Regardless of your answer, cologne is a very tricky gift. What for one person is a raging turn-on can sometimes be severely off-putting to another. A fine illustration of this point would be the words "jock odor."

Sharing a big bottle of bubbly says:
(a) This is to celebrate our relationship.
(b) This is to get me drunk so you look better.
(c) This is to wash down the rufies.

If you answered (c), this is not a good sign. No matter how ugly you think you are, you do not need drugs to get someone, just better lighting. Or perhaps none. There is a reason back rooms are dark.

Dining at home by candlelight is:
(a) Wonderfully romantic.
(b) Good for hiding the mess you never cleaned up.
(c) Sad because, well, it's just you there, isn't it?

If you answered (c), congratulations; you're better off than you know. You don't have to stress over any of this Valentine mess. You can stop reading this piece and call up www.gaycyberslut/singlesofuckit.com right now.

The gift of hard-to-find hand-milled French soap says:
(a) When you bathe, you deserve the best.
(b) When you want me to do that thing you like, I don't wanna gag.
(c) When you come home after staying late at the office, you better the hell smell like this.

Ah, the issue of trust. If you give a loaded gift like this, you have work to do on your relationship. If you are given a gift like this, keep at least one piece of it handy in the car.

Giving a card—just a card—says:
(a) I forgot.
(b) I'm cheap.
(c) It doesn't matter because either way you can expect to be dumped pronto.

I mean really, a *card*? An insurance agent will send you a card. The only way a card will do is if it says something thoughtful, poetic, romantically inspired, and truly meaningful, like:

> Roses are red,
> Swiss cheese has holes,
> I sold a kidney
> To buy you a Rolls.

Now you're beginning to get to point. Have a happy Valentine's Day, and I'll see you in the poorhouse. If not the doghouse.

PART SEVEN
Going Places

AND AWAY WE GO

The trouble with gay travel is that it just isn't gay. Oh, there are gay cruises and the like, but they're just the regular thing, only packed with homos and better entertainment—not all of it onstage. I'm talking about boring, normal, everyday travel.

Flying is made tolerable due to the fleets of gay male flight attendants. Every now and then a straight one slips through, though. On my last flight I noticed one because his wedding band was on his left hand. When I confronted him in outrage he broke down. "It's true," he wept, "but please don't tell anyone; I really need this job." I got an upgrade and drank free all the way to New York. Yes, the actual flying part is OK; it's the airport that's so miserable.

Part of the problem is that there are just so darn many straight people to deal with. At the ticket counter, at the check-in, in the overpriced food stalls; I don't mean to alarm you, but they're everywhere. Especially at the security station, where you would not believe how judgmental they can get over an innocent little cock ring. I believe with a little coaxing, a few beers, and proper lighting, a cavity search could be made entertaining. But not here. We need our own airline, big enough to merit its own terminal. We would call it TWGay Airlines.

TWGay would have all certifiably gay male flight attendants, and I would get to do the certifying. The pilot and ground crew would be lesbians because, let's face it, gays make things fun, lesbians get things done. I can imagine me in the pilot's seat: "What do you mean, there's no reverse? How do we parallel park?"

On a TWGay flight you'd be on an airplane where once cruising altitude was reached, actual cruising would begin. That boring speech before takeoff would be different too. "In the event of an emergency, grab the person you've been flirting with and do what you want because unless you're the pilot, there's nothing you can do, so you may as well be going down going down."

Have you ever spent time in one of those first class airport lounges? It's where rich people drink the same bad coffee that's served in the concourse but feel smug and superior about it because it's in a china cup. You can get free candy bars and a newspaper too, which is a savings of maybe $1.25, and all for paying two to three times the coach fare. Most unforgivable, though, is that *it's boring*! The TWGay lounge would feature a dance floor, lockers, a steam room, and a maze. If you have to kill time at the airport, you might as well have a good time doing it.

Let's say you've arrived at one of the most popular vacation destinations—a theme park. Can it be considered gay? Depends on where you went.

Disneyland/World is already so gay, all it needs to advertise the fact is an overtly gay-themed ride like, say, Pirates of the Caribbean. Oh. Never mind.

Six Flags theme parks are so hetero it's disturbing, but that's what you get for building them in places like Texas and Valencia. Someone needs to remind them that their mascot, Bugs Bunny, leaps into women's clothing every chance he gets.

Sea World–type parks are more about nature than rides or mascots. There's always the tank full of fish that change sex as circumstances demand. One wonders what Pat Robertson would think of that. Can't you just see right-wingers picketing against "ungodly" fish? Wait till they learn about those hermaphroditic sponges, the ones that provide both sperm and egg, becoming single parents to millions of little spongettes.

I love these kinds of parks because they're about nature and nature is all about diversity; just look at us. I will admit a twinge of irritation that penguins are by and large heterosexual. You'd think more would be gay given how nicely they dress. Speaking of dressing, I hate any park or zoo that demeans its animals by making them wear human clothes. You know some straight person came up with that. No gay in the world would say, "Hey, let's put a dress on a monkey and see if he looks good." And they call us perverts? No, honey, regardless of what animals you have, if there are going to be outrageous costumes on stage, gay men are going to be the ones wearing them. Three words: Siegfried and Roy.

Which brings me to the subject of Las Vegas. With all the exotic resorts being built there, you'd think we'd have one of our own. Something like Key West West or West Hollywood East or, simply, the Castro Casino, where when you play the slots you pull an entirely different kind of handle. The nightclub at the top would be called P-town and getting there would entail walking a dark and winding path from the elevators through the Pines. The obligatory mall would be made up of stores like Don't Panic, International Male, a Colt Gallery, a Tom of Finland store, and Restoration Hardware. Oh, and a Disney Store, of course.

In the Womyn's Wing, instead of Cirque du Soleil in permanent residence there would be Lilith Fair. Their mall would include stores that sold Birkenstocks, candles, crystals, and anything you'd ever want for cats. Tattoos and piercing would be free for any guest staying in a first-class suite or spending over $500 in the Dungeon, the interactive exploratorium where you go in vanilla and come out kinky— *if* you come out.

And of course you would have to "come out" to enjoy either the airline or the Vegas resort. Not that I want to discriminate against our own, but nobody wants to party with people wrapped up in fear, self-loathing, and clothes from Sears. If this is you, honey, you really do need a holiday. Let me urge you to leave behind all that repression, the living of the lie, and those invitations to way too many wedding and baby showers. It's high time you threw on a Carmen Miranda hat and lived your life for nobody but you.

Now *that* would be a vacation.

HI HO, THE GLAMOROUS LIFE

I've always loved traveling. I got the bug for it in 1980. I was right out of college and touring with a group that performed theater for young people, imaginatively called Theater for Young People. We spent four months playing every city, small town, crossroads, and pig path in North Carolina on a per diem of $20. That 20 bucks had to cover meals, road necessities, *and* lodging. In order not to exceed our per diem we ended up staying in some interesting places.

Outside of Lenoir, N.C., we stayed at a dump of a motel where the walls were so thin a drunken trucker fell through his bathroom into one of the women's rooms. He apologized profusely and exited by crashing through a window. Thinking fast, the ladies ran for the manager, not to call the police but to make him give them the room for free. I'm telling you, that per diem was precious.

We had a week's residency in Sparta, N.C., at their one high school. For some reason their team was not the Spartans but the Trojans. That should have tipped us off we were in for something different. Instead of a motel, they put us up on the outskirts of town in the hospital wing of a low-security juvenile correctional facility. We had the same curfew and lights-out as the inmates but what the hell, we could handle anything if it meant saving some of that per diem. Besides, deep down the kids weren't so bad, just angry at having been abused and abandoned. We liked them so we gave them a couple of free workshops. Mistake! Being starved for attention, they went nuts for us. We couldn't go anywhere there without being mobbed. We were the Beatles of Sparta. These poor sad kids loved us so much they broke curfew by the dozens to sneak into our antiseptic hospital rooms to talk to us about our glamorous lives and offer us free pot. We were worried they'd get busted for the curfew, not to mention the pot, so we kept shooing them out and locking the doors. That did no good because they were, after all, delinquents, and a locked door was merely a challenge. In two minutes they picked the locks and tumbled back in with grins, contraband Sara Lee cake, and a bong. Panic was setting in with us. All we needed was to get caught with a roomful of underage kids with criminal records and marijuana on our beds wearing only their underwear. We begged them not to spark the bong and they agreed, but only if we would perform one of our shows for them. In a further effort to avoid getting them in trouble, we ended up sneaking into their dorms to do it so they wouldn't get caught off-limits in ours. We have to be the only people ever to have broken *into* a correctional facility.

In Bryson City we stayed down the street from a charming little traveling carnival. After we checked into our motel, we went down to the carnival and spent 50 cents each to ride an Indian elephant in the mountains of North Carolina. It was magical. The spell was broken the next morning when we discovered the guy who had the elephant was staying at our motel. More to the point, the elephant was staying at our motel. She was kept in an enormous cage on a flatbed in the parking lot. Being a neat elephant and not wanting to clutter her space, she had backed against the bars to do her sizable business. The next morning we found the way to our van, which was parked adjacent, naturally, paved with soccer ball–size elephant poop. None of us ate breakfast that morning.

One night near Fuquay-Varina (and that's "*fyoo*-kway"

in case you were wondering) my roommate and I were next door to a room where there was considerable action. Being moral, well-bred young men, we were shocked to hear such wanton sex and went straight to the manager. We demanded one glass apiece, then raced back and put them against the wall, the better to hear every lurid detail. There were two women and two men in the next door room. One of the men, named Derek, was attempting something with Candy, who found it extremely uncomfortable and complained loudly. The other woman, Cherry, and the other man, who was called—I swear to God—Tiny, were coaxing Candy on.

"You can do it, baby," Cherry coached, "Breathe!"

This continued for about an hour. Every so often Cherry would cuss at Candy and demonstrate, albeit with difficulty, how it was supposed to be done. Derek grew irritated at these demonstrations, urgently wishing her to fully complete the maneuver. Cherry was adamant, though, insisting to Candy that she "do what you come here to do." I remember thinking that whatever this could possibly be, it might be advisable to start with someone named Tiny. At one point there was shouting and a scuffle, and the door was thrown open. We rushed to the curtains. Candy was in the gravel parking lot, bare-assed and cursing like fourth-generation tobacco trash. Cherry ran out after her in a ratty see-through peignoir screaming in a voice like a fork in the disposal, "What is wrong with you?" She threw a coat over the otherwise naked Candy, demanding, "Ain't you got no *decency*?" Back inside a deal was brokered between all parties. Amends were made with Cherry doing the honors and an equitable—not to mention enthusiastically loud—conclusion met. Twice. You go, Tiny.

The next morning, as we piled into our van, Kate, one of the girls on our tour who had the room on the other side of us asked, "What the hell kind of TV show were you watching last night?" I told her we'd been watching real people. "I

hate that show," she said, "but I do like *That's Incredible*."
Given Candy's and even Cherry's difficulty accommodating
Derek, it might have been that too.

NEW YORK ON NEXT TO NOTHING

Fred and I shared a one-room apartment in Manhattan at the corner of 56th and Third with another couple. We were all four in a comedy group called Gross National Product, and the leader, Tom, had taken up with Janice, the woman who leased the apartment. When Fred and I moved up from Washington, D.C., he bamboozled her into allowing us to share this tiny and not at all private space with them. The upside was we didn't have far to go for rehearsals; the downside was, it was so cramped and our lives so exposed that there occurred far more drama than comedy. It didn't help that Janice was certifiable and Tom insanely manic.

The apartment was on the second floor over a Ray Bari's Pizza, so naturally we had mice. When we cooked anything in the oven we would see them fleeing across the floor. After much debate we bought traps and set them all over. At night we would hear SNAP!—scuffle scuffle scuffle...scuffle. Scuffle. And then Janice sobbing. Tom would leap up in verminary triumph, fling the entire mousetrap and victim in the trash, and gleefully sketch another mouse head with a line through it on the kitchen area wall. Over time he ran out of space and had to start a second and then third line of mouse heads.

Eventually, Janice could take this no longer and moved out of her own apartment. Tom, however, convinced her to let us illegally sublet and continued seeing her. None of us had money. We would have rice with soy sauce and call it "eating Chinese." Most dinners were variations on butter noodles and cookies we bought at the Smilers market across the street. The glamour of the Big Apple was distinctly absent.

You could live on minimum wage in North Carolina. We had even made do on it in the suburbs of D.C. Manhattan was another matter. I worked in a long two-aisle paperback bookstore on Lexington across from Hunter College making, yes, minimum wage. We carried books assigned by the professors at Hunter. Idiot students would come in and ask for "that Shakespeare play about love." "That narrows the field," I would say, dripping in wasted sarcasm, roiling with resentment. Then I'd hand them *Romeo and Juliet* and overcharge them.

Three months into the job my boss allowed me to take the deposit to the bank around the corner. He acted as if he were bestowing a weighty honor upon me. The way he handed me the tattered lunch bag with cash and checks inside, you'd have thought I was receiving the keys to heaven. I took it dully and did the chore, wondering how I could stretch it into an hour as the teller added up the checks and counted the money. "You're $20 over," she said, handing back two tens with the receipt. I couldn't believe it. My boss was testing my honesty. His obvious and clumsy manner infuriated me— until I realized this was a godsend. If I pocketed the money, he wouldn't say anything but he'd know I couldn't be trusted. If I returned it he'd believe me scrupulously honest and never bother keeping an eye on me again. I went directly back to the store and gave him the $20. He beamed. So did I.

For the rest of the time I worked there I was able to pilfer from the cash register. I would take customers' money but not ring up the sales. That way the cash drawer always balanced out. My boss was a nice man who liked me, and when I stole I felt more vile than the rodents in our apartment, but at least this rat could now afford to eat meat. One does what one must in the city.

Meanwhile, Fred was working at Bloomingdale's in the

Polo section, also at minimum wage. They made him wear a suit and tie, which he couldn't afford. It meant buying clothes at decidedly downscale Alexander's so you could sell clothes at outrageously overpriced Bloomingdale's. Celebrities shop at Bloomie's, and since Fred knows who everybody is in show business, he was in heaven, at least at the beginning. He waited on the teacher from the movie *My Bodyguard,* which had come out three years earlier, and she was flattered by the recognition. "So what are you doing now?" he asked. Apparently it was not the question to ask. I'm guessing it still isn't because you ain't seen her in nothing since.

A week or two later Fred saw Sylvester Stallone wander through in a floor-length coat of dead chinchillas (harking back to our minor theme of rodents). Just in case anyone was missing the point, he was actually whistling the theme from *Rocky.* He stayed long enough for everyone to notice and then swept away like Cruella De Vil in drag.

One day Jack Nicholson, who was appearing in *Terms of Endearment* at the movies across the street, walked in with a bimbo who picked out the worst possible shirts for him. It was back when Polo was conning hefty straight men into buying wide horizontal stripes in electric blue and yellow or hot pink and purple. I think we all knew we were in for trouble when Ralph Lauren married a woman. Anyway, these were the shirts the bimbo was pulling out. Fred couldn't take it any longer, feeling forced to play Fashion Police. He walked up to the Oscar-winning international star and told him the shirts made him look fat. "Mr. Nicholson, I am a large person too, so take it from me, you do not want to wear these." He braced for the legendary wrath, thinking, "Is this worth it for minimum wage?" Instead, Mr. Nicholson flashed the famous "inches from a clean getaway" smile and said, "Well, then, what would you suggest?" The bimbo fumed behind him. Fred picked out a couple of less expensive, darker solids, and Mr. Nicholson bought an even dozen while the bimbo stood behind the star mouthing "fuck you" over and over at Fred. Jack Nicholson shook Fred's hand and left. The furious bimbo came over and hissed, "You work in Bloomingdale's, you little faggot." "Yes, I do," he replied, "but at least I can tell my parents what I do for a living. By the way, your meal ticket's leaving, and I suggest you follow." Then he gave her his broadest smile, adding, "Have a nice day, you cunting bitch whore." Watching her seething off after the star, Fred realized the real pisser was that her line of work paid far more than his. Oh well, at least he'd met someone famous.

Fred got over the whole celebrity thing, though, the day Jaclyn Smith changed her kid's full diaper on his counter. Fred stood there appalled and aghast. The topper was when she asked if he could throw it away for her. "*No.*" And thus, Fred was out of work with a bad suit.

Next to the Ray Bari's below us was a glorified muffin and omelet shop called Our Miss Brooks. The woman at the register circumvented her minimum wage life by having a friend come by and "rob" her every so often. It got a little obvious when he started asking for coffee. Fred happened to be in there when she was fired, so he applied for the job. It was still minimum wage, but he could sleep until ten minutes before he had to be there, and it came with breakfast. Of course we all went there for free food. Unfortunately, it was awful. The management cared so little about their omelets that they actually made Fred chef. As a cook he can make a great cup of coffee, but it ends there.

While our comedy group was performing on West 82nd Street, my money got so low I was forced to call in all debts I was owed by friends. I told them I would comp them for the Thursday show if they would pay me what they owed. That night I had my fortune restored—$26. Everyone else in the show was going out, but I was taking my cache of cash safely home. Waiting for the subway at 86th, I got mugged at knifepoint by two men who beat me up and relieved me of all the money I had in the world. When the police finally arrived they asked where the cop assigned to this station was. He showed up on cue, hustling and out of breath with, I swear to God, powdered doughnut all down his front. The other cops asked if I wanted a ride home. I refused in angry defiance. This was my town, damn it, and no one was going to take it away through fear. In a grand gesture, Doughnut Boy bought me a conciliatory token. "Thanks," I said, "this makes up for everything. Next time get glazed."

Around this time Tom broke up with Janice because she kept attempting suicide. She didn't take it well. After she spent a week in Bellevue our sublet sort of fell through. Fred and I couldn't afford a place on our own, and we couldn't find anyone who could take two people as roommates, so we were forced to find separate places to live. I moved in with Donnie, a college buddy, who was illegally subletting a cubicle on West 89th. Donnie was an actor, which meant he also was broke. For rent he worked as a cater waiter, which was good money but only on the weekends. Stretched over the days between jobs, it was very like minimum wage. The only perk in catering is uneaten food. Donnie brought home armloads of uneaten catered food, almost all of it desserts. In our Gotham penury we ate entire meals of glacéed fruit tarts, blancmange, cannoli, Linzer tortes, napoleons, panettone, and puff pastries with whipped cream piped onto them so they looked like swans. Afterward, for entertainment, we would fill Big Gulp cups with $4-a-gallon wine, go to the park, and hoot at the men with increasing loudness until the cops made us leave. We're lucky to be alive.

On the other side of town, Fred had actually managed to set a cheese omelet on fire, which might have been forgivable had it not spread to his manager. So it was that Fred entered the world of telemarketing. He was calling up innocent people to push something called the Sweet Pickles' Pre-School Program of Books. A major hurdle was just pronouncing the product name again and again. It was torture on both ends of the line. He begged his temp company to move him to another part of telemarketing hell, and was sent to Dun & Bradstreet. There he didn't have to sell anything. All he had to do was call D&B customers and teach them how to use the company's intricate automated financial information system. The people he called were primarily technophobic entry-level bean counters who were unlikely to use the system anyway, so it wasn't terribly important that Fred be accurate. He relaxed and almost enjoyed the gig.

At that job he became buddies with a guy who was sort of Big Temp on Campus, being the first hired temp and overseer of newer temps such as Fred. BTOC had the hots for the D&B woman who was in charge of all the temps, including him. She returned his hots. Fred saw an opportunity, lent them the use of his apartment, and off these two went, regularly, to commingle funds. For his part, Fred got the friendship of BTOC and a D&B boss who happily tacked oh, so many extra hours onto his time sheets. This went on for a good while, very like *The Apartment*, except Jack Lemmon's apartment wasn't a shared sublet. One day Fred's roommate came home early to find two strangers having sex on his sofa. A scene ensued, peace officers arrived, and, well, all good things must come to an end.

Interestingly, we ran into BTOC years later in Los Angeles at a party. For several years he had been a beloved sitcom costar on one of those long-running shows you wonder why they keep on year after year. Still, he remembered Fred fondly. He's married now with a beautiful child, and, one assumes, no more assignations on Jennifer Convertibles.

But back to being poor.

I was sick of the bookstore, so I borrowed money from my brother to learn typing and word processing at the YWCA. I was desperate to get myself a decent temp job. I landed a secretary gig in the financial district by stealing Donnie's cater waiter jacket and some of Fred's ties from his Bloomie's days. I had to take the Broadway line all the way downtown, trains so crowded I regularly rode between the cars with other low-level Wall Street gofers in dingy white short-sleeve shirts, shiny pants, and skinny ties. I worked as a secretary for the person-nel director of Dow Jones. I believed she was a lesbian because she had short butch hair, kicked ass, and had everyone but me living in fear of her. I loved her immediately, and we got along famously. This job taught me the power of being a temp. People assume a temp has an IQ roughly equivalent to the temperature of thawing meat. If you can show up on time, answer a phone, and construct a sentence, they treat you like you're the greatest thing since collated copying. I worked at a snail's pace, but the important stuff got done, with all the grammar corrected too. I was offered three different perma-nent positions there but turned them down because I wanted to stay free to perform our comedy. I could have had a job like Tess in *Working Girl* that came with a 401(k) that would have seen me on world cruises in my golden years, but I would have become boring, which is the eighth deadly sin, and died long before my heart gave out.

So Fred and I continued temping and doing the show. Our comedy group couldn't get paid bookings in New York, but the folks in D.C. wanted us back. The schedule was grueling. I'd work Monday through a half day Friday, cram into a rental car with Fred, Tom, a womanizing, alcoholic British expatriate, a woman who was Janice's replacement, and another woman whose mother had a place in Chevy Chase where we could crash. We would drive down to Washington, where we would perform once that night and twice on Saturday, drive back up on Sunday, and start the whole thing over again the next week. This went on for the months of July and August. During the two most miserably hot months of the year we were schlepping between the two most miserably humid cities in creation.

In New York during the week, Tom spent months pitching HBO all of our ideas for shows and programming. He was like an overly enthusiastic yet highly entertaining dog you keep batting away that relentlessly comes back. Week after week they kept telling us, "We'll see what the guys on the Coast say." Being so gung ho, we didn't recognize the brush-off. Being naïve in the extreme we decided to hell with these people, let's move out to the Coast and pitch them directly.

And so over time we left New York one by one, switching coasts. The amount of culture shock was unexpected and surprisingly rough. I missed New York so much I refused to allow myself a visit until I got over it. That wasn't a difficult vow to keep as my income in Los Angeles ensured I would not be visiting anywhere for a very long time. Still, I would think of the City.

New York is the dirtiest, ugliest, most dangerous, rat-infested, beautiful, glittering, appalling, tough, exciting, stimulating, oppressive, piss-soaked, sexy, grim, gritty, gorgeous, overwhelming, awesome, noisy, unsavory, pushy, marvelous, insane, intense, unsympathetic, inspiring, kinetic, insufferable, intrusive, hard-edged, hellish, glorious, fractious, fascinating, exuberant, perverse, exquisite, draining, disturbing, extreme, creative, confrontive, brilliant, amazing, bewildering, and thrilling place I know. It's the greatest place on earth to visit.

And you couldn't pay me to live there again. At least not on minimum wage.

WHATEVER FLOATS YOUR BOAT

Years ago Fred and I decided to visit California's lovely Catalina Island. If you ever go, sign up for all the cheesy tours you can, especially the Glass-Bottom Boat and Flying Fish Tours. The Flying Fish Tour is at night, which gives you plenty of time to recover from the Glass-Bottom Boat Tour. You'll need it; here's why.

Aboard the Glass-Bottom Boat you've got your head between your knees, looking down through a distorted panel in the boat's bottom into undulating water on a rolling ocean. Are you getting the picture? Through sheer will I was doing OK—and then the boat started to move. It is not a large boat, and the bottom is flat, so there is much rocking. After about five minutes of this, there was also pitching—mainly from the kids on board, although there was a spectacular eruption from an ample adult. We were treated to a second viewing as it passed beneath us. The tour guides are used to this and did not stop their educational spiel. Did you know those beautiful golden Garibaldi fish eat such garbage that when they die other fish won't eat them? Only crabs will clean them up, and I understand they charge a hefty service fee. Think about that the next time you're having crab salad.

Back on land and two margaritas later I was feeling much better. I decided it was the head between my knees part that had made it so bad. Well, that and the fried onion loaf with scampi for lunch. Still, if I'm ever in an airplane emergency and told to put my head between my knees, forget it. I may

end up a grease spot in a cornfield, but I'm not gonna be nauseous getting there.

When the sun went down it was time for the Flying Fish
Tour. The flying fish off Catalina are the world's largest,
growing to around 18 inches in length, and they gather in the
deep water off the island at night. I thought they flew 'cuz it
was cool. Turns out the noise of the boat's engine frightens
the fish so much that they burst out of the water in a heart-
stopping adrenaline panic. Learning we were terrifying them
into flying made me feel rude and unnecessarily disruptive,
like showing my aunt Helen a copy of *Stunt Butt* magazine
just to watch her have conniptions—fun to watch but totally
uncalled for. A truly terrorized fish can travel 35 miles per
hour and glide over 100 feet. Thanks to the powerful search-
light on the boat we were able to see horrified hundreds.
When we got to the far end of the tour, the guide shone the
light on a narrow beach covered in seals. The seals did exactly what you would do if someone turned a spotlight on you
while you were trying to sleep. They jostled and barked, and
I swear one of them gave us the flipper. Clearly, this tour was
about alarming marine life.

On the way back we threw blind fear into more flying
fish, and, inevitably, one flew into the boat. It hit a wholly
unprepared woman squarely in the neck. What did this group
of 35 concerned fellow human beings do when we witnessed
this unfortunate event? We laughed in great howls, pointed,
and hooted. Fred thought he was going to wet his pants. This
poor woman was going to have a welt that would take a great
deal of explaining Monday morning. Added to that, this two-
pound flying fish had slithered all down her dress. You may
know that fish are covered with slime, but flying fish slime is
particularly pungent. The woman reeked, and all of us were
quite merry about it the entire way back, including her husband. That was a man who, no doubt, would be sleeping in
the garage until Christmas. Even today, all Fred or I have to

do is imitate Woman Hit in Neck by Flying Fish to cause the other to convulse in tears of laughter. Perhaps I shouldn't be so proud of that.

Catalina gave us terrific memories, which was great because our previous oceanic excursions had not gone so well. Several months prior, Fred and I had been hosting a friend from Florida named Brynn who after five days had worn out his welcome in several ways. More about that later. While mediating tensions between Fred and Brynn, I was struck by a brilliant idea: Let's all go whale watching! What was I thinking?

We arrived at the water's edge on a beautiful afternoon with a bracing breeze. Just before we cast off, a Brownie Troop showed up. Hell is being on a 40-foot boat overrun with screaming little girls. Fred, who was never completely sold on this whale watching idea anyway, was already irritable, queasy, and bent on letting me know about it for the rest of the trip. Twenty minutes out Brynn became nauseous too. He was fighting it by sitting behind the pilothouse and staring at it fixedly so he couldn't see the rocking of the boat. It worked just dandy too until the second mate came out, sat across from him, and tore open a pickled egg sandwich. Fish were fed.

I was fine the entire trip, running all over the boat like Queequeg singing sea chanteys. I found Fred up on the top deck and, in my best Pirates of the Caribbean, growled, "Argh, matey, the wind's a-pickin' up!" Fred, shivering and urpy, was not amused. With the wind came a heaving ocean, pun intended. The Brownies got sick en masse. Unfortunately, it was not along the bottom rail where damage would have been minimal, but from the top deck. Those on the bottom deck, Brynn included, rushed toward the center and away from the sides, but it was no use. The wind blew it everywhere.

Brynn came up top shaking Brownie Chow off his jacket.

"When do we get back to land?" he whined. "This is the worst trip I've ever had, you guys. Look at this, peas and corn. This was a terrible idea. I wish I were back in Florida."

Fred stood, and I could tell he had snapped. "*You* wish you were back in Florida!" he said loudly in Brynn's face. "Who was it that, while we were at work, rewired our entertainment center so he could dub copies of *Lick 'Em Clean, Good Will Sucking,* and *Anal Mania* parts 1 through 5?" We had the full attention of a shocked den mother and a dozen Brownies with crusty chins, but Fred was on a roll. "And who went tricking on Saturday night, bringing a potential murderer into our house?"

"Oh, he wouldn't hurt a fly; he was only 16."

"Sixteen!" I screeched in horror. If I'd known that when I walked in on them, I'd have stopped them immediately instead of watching for 20 minutes first. "Brynn, you realize we could be talking rape here?"

"Tell me about it. I'm not used to being a bottom."

"That's it. Out!" shouted Fred. "I want your jailbait chicken-chasing ass out of my house, I want *Daddy's Whore Boys* out of my VCR, and I want you and your rosy raw rectum *out of my life!*"

There followed a mortified silence broken at last by a girl's thin, sweet voice. "Mrs. Lamb, what's a whore boy?"

All in all I thought it went well. We made it back to shore without Fred throwing Brynn overboard, Brynn packed up his pirated porno and departed that evening, never to call again, and I overheard the Den Mother explaining that "war boys" are military men engaged in heavy action. I saw the video, and, you know, she was right on the money.

WHAT I DID ON MY SUMMER VACATION

Last summer my partner, Fred, and I went to Florida for our vacation. "Disney World in *August*," you shriek. "*What* were you thinking?" Well, the Southern Baptists weren't going, and we felt it was up to us to fill the gap, although Fred went a tad overboard. Disney stock gained three points on what he purchased alone.

We hit the park primed to battle any and all to see the Parade of Hercules, although once we found out Herc wears a fake muscle suit the fight went out of us. The parade route was lined with quite a wall of flesh anyway as Disney World seems to attract truly enormous people. So instead we lounged among Fred's purchases in the shade of a woman from Virginia. Forgoing the Parade of Hercules we watched the crowd, which we dubbed the Parade of Imminent Coronary Blockage. We made a grim game of identifying those within days of turning to their mate and saying "Lurlene, muh arm's gone numb."

I insisted we do the Haunted Mansion for the gayest reason I know: The wallpaper is fabulous. The scariest thing there, though, was a family from, I swear to God, Stump, Miss., consisting of what sounded like Lurloo, Stick, Mump, Boomer, Me-Maw and Pee-Pop. We were drawn into conversation when Baby ("We ain't named it yet") vomited down the back of my leg. They told us they come every year but were disappointed this time because 20,000 Leagues Under the Sea was closed and it was Boomer's favorite. I was trying to imagine Boomer fitting down the hatch when Stick let slip that they were Southern Baptists and weren't supposed to be there at all. We told them it was all right; we were gay, and if it got out that we were talking to them, we'd lose our membership too. They didn't care much about the boycott because "Uncle Stubby is 'that way' too." I smiled politely, thanking my lucky stars I was not a gay man named Stubby.

Disney World has two shows about going back in time and two about traveling in space, and experiencing them, I noticed some interesting things. Paul "Pee-wee" Reubens is the voice of the robot in Star Tours. Alien Encounter stars Tim "Rocky Horror" Curry and features Jeffrey "Ed Wood" Jones and that great Friend of Queers Kathy Najimy. The Timekeeper, a Circle Vision attraction about time travel, features two robots: One is a fey, prissy thing voiced by Robin Williams in high *Birdcage;* the other is a butch contraption voiced by Rhea Perlman. Together they manage to come off as the biggest gay/dyke mechanical pairing since C3PO and R2D2. The Universe of Energy ride back to the Cenozoic era is hosted by Ellen DeGeneres and Bill Nye, the Science Guy, who is not gay but is cute in a geeky sort of way. Plus he sports a nice basket in those shorts as he tromps through dinosaur dioramas. Now, what do all these gay influences tell us in terms of future science? If you're gonna travel through time or space, you're gonna need yourself some homos. My proof is the ride Body Wars, which is stupid, confusing, and dull. But what would you expect from an attraction starring Elizabeth "Cocktail" Shue and Tim "Animal House" Matheson?

By afternoon we had learned how to cope with the long lines: Pick out an attractive guy, follow him, and get in whichever line he joins. If you're going to be staring at the back of someone for an hour, it may as well be someone you can spend the time fantasizing over. I have a bent for hunky young fathers, which meant I spent most of my day in line for Mr. Toad's Wild Ride and Peter Pan's Flight—another instance of flight accomplished by a fairy, thank you.

Speaking of, where were all the homosexuals? I mean, besides those running the rides. We decided that most gays know better than to go to family theme parks in Florida in the middle of August. We counted 14 gay men and two lesbians that day for a ratio of seven to one, which proves to me that lesbians are seven times smarter than gay men.

Back at the hotel we checked out the pool. Too many kids and not enough dads. Back in our room, Fred inventoried our purchases and decided he needed to go downstairs to buy not one, but two more suitcases to contain them. When Fred returned I'd fallen asleep. God bless him, I awoke to room service. Being married is great.

The next day we shifted to EPCOT, unaware of how tired we were becoming. We had gotten cranky and dismissive of attractions with utterly vague names. What the hell is Horizons? What genius came up with Wonders of Life and the completely uninspired The Land? I told Fred I fully expected to see one labeled Stuff. Fred, who'd had it with the humidity and crowds, said he was hoping to find one called Someplace Else. But we were in Disney World, damn it, so we couldn't leave yet. We limited our search to those attractions we really wanted to find: The Hall of No Children and The Pavilion of Air-Conditioning. Instead, we found The Restaurant of Great Tumult and Din at The American Adventure. The adventure consisted of battling for bad food and getting to a table without being trampled. It was during this meal, about the third time one of us was smeared with ice cream from a passing child, that we decided to leave Walt Disney World and spend the rest of our time with friends in Jacksonville.

Which is what we should have done in the first place. Next year we shall go someplace without gift stores featuring porcelain Disney villains and all-too-handy ATMs. It will be a spot that is remote, cool, and without children. Next year, expect a postcard from Antarctica.

PART EIGHT
The Arts

KISSES ON YOUR OPENING

I was at a party where five gay men were hotly debating the merits of our favorite musicals. A lesbian came in, listened for a few moments, then asked, "What's *Dreamgirls*?" The room went silent. To get the ball rolling again she asked if we had seen last night's game. We looked at each other until one man asked, "You mean *Jeopardy*?" His partner added, "Oh, I saw that, can you believe not one of the three got any of the 'Musical Theater' category right?" "I blame our educational system," said another. "There is no appreciation of history in this country." We were off and running again. The lesbian shook her head and went looking for someone who did not think a "long bomb" was *Mame* with Lucille Ball.

I've heard it said that gay men are born with either the musical gene or the Madonna gene. There's nothing wrong with the Madonna just-wanna-dance gene. Mine's there; it's just recumbent. I got the musical gene big time, though. It's not hard to see why so many of us have it. As a boy growing up in the land of Jesse Helms I spent a lot of fantasy time listening to people sing about people they weren't supposed to love. "We Kiss in a Shadow," "I Loved You Once In Silence," heck, everything in *West Side Story*. I got my frustrations out by lip-synching to "Rose's Turn" from *Gypsy*. I choreographed the better part of South Pacific in our living room. I staged the entire second act of *I Do! I Do!* with my two cats. And all that was just last week.

We musical theater queens are a passionate bunch.

Want blood? Start a debate over Stephen Sondheim versus
Andrew Lloyd Webber. Say Harold Prince is a hack. Opine
that Michael Bennett may not have been God. We are
equally bitchy about anything we don't like. For instance:
Give me the gun, Rolf, *I'll* take care of those stinking Von
Trapp brats.

There are obvious ways to tell whether you have the
musical gene. Is it impossible for you to make an entrance
without striking a pose and hearing "One!—singular sensation" from *A Chorus Line* in your head? Can you recognize
a show that ran six performances just by the intro to its most
obscure number? When you do your Paul Lynde impression,
is it a quip from the old *Hollywood Squares* or "Kids" from
Bye Bye Birdie? Do you own *Les Miserables* in English,
French, Dutch, Icelandic, and Tagalog? Do you wonder whatever happened to Tommy Steele? When you think of *42nd
Street,* do you think of prostitutes or tap dancing? (If you
think of tap-dancing prostitutes, that's *The Life* and you've
definitely got the gene.) If you're still not sure, I've devised the
following test.

In the movie musical *Gigi* who sings "Thank Heaven For
Little Girls?"
(a) Ellen DeGeneres.
(b) Woody Allen.
(c) Maurice Chevalier.

In *Dreamgirls* Jennifer Holliday sang "And I Am Telling
You I'm Not...
(a) "Taking Down the Marky Mark Poster."
(b) "A Model For Weight Watchers."
(c) "Going."

The aria "Glitter and Be Gay" is from:
(a) *The RuPaul Show.*

(b) Harvey Fierstein's presidential campaign (hey, it could happen).

(c) *Candide.*

In "The Ladies Who Lunch" from *Company* a tipsy Elaine Stritch asked "Does anybody still wear...?

(a) "Old Spice."

(b) "Condoms."

(c) "A hat."

"Slide Some Oil to Me" is sung by:

(a) Jeff Stryker in *Solo Shots #4.*

(b) Captain Joseph Hazelwood of the Exxon Valdez.

(c) The Tin Man in *The Wiz.*

Complete the lyric "There are big-busted women..."

(a) "Coming out of clinics in Beverly Hills."

(b) "Cluttering the beach on *Baywatch.*

(c) "Over the wall" from *Kiss of the Spider Woman.*

The worst thing ever to happen to Broadway was:

(a) The Great Depression.

(b) World War II.

(c) *Cats.*

The scariest musical Broadway ever gave us was:

(a) Len Cariou slitting throats in *Sweeney Todd.*

(b) Betty Buckley terrorizing her daughter in the short-lived *Carrie.*

(c) Carol Channing touring in *Hello, Dolly!* Again.

Complete the phrase "You got trouble, right here in..."

(a) "The Buttonwillow rest stop."

(b) "Your prostate."

(c) "River City" from *The Music Man.*

"I Enjoy Being a Girl" is sung by:
(a) Half the gay male population on Halloween.
(b) Marv Albert.
(c) Nancy Kwan in *Flower Drum Song*.

Bonus Question:
Of the musicals *Jekyll & Hyde*, *The Scarlet Pimpernel*, and *The Civil War*, which did Frank Wildhorn *not* write on a coffee break?
(This is a trick question. He wrote them all on a coffee break—the *same* coffee break.)

OK, forget the scoring, the right answers are all (c). So if you didn't get it or you are still unsure, you're not a musical theater queen. For instance, if you think Jerome Robbins played third base for the Giants, you are not an MTQ. If you think *Nine* is merely a desirable length, you are not an MTQ. And you are definitely not an MTQ if you think Kander and Ebb were the comedy team on *Hee Haw*.

No, not everybody is a musical theater queen, and that's perfectly all right. It's less about attending shows than approaching life with verve, flair, and, whenever possible, a costume out of *Follies*. We need drama and fun and a truly terrific score (and no, I'm not talking about that usher you did backstage). We need more talented costars in our lives and a chorus to back us up. We need good lighting, direction and a better script. All of this can be found at the theater, just don't leave it there along with your program when the house lights come up. Remember, whoever you are, you're a star, honey, so sing out, Louise!

UNTIL *WHAT* FAT LADY SINGS?

Fred and I recently watched a documentary about a primitive tribal ritual wherein the elders take blows to the head as a sign of their ability to withstand pain. Fred remarked that in the Western world we call this opera. Need I add that any operas I have seen I have seen alone?

To be honest, I have hugely ambivalent feelings about opera. In such enormous productions there are so many things that can go wrong. Often the first and biggest, for me, is purchasing a ticket. And yet I go. I climb to my very cheap seat in the Dorothy Chandler Pavilion and, reeling from thin oxygen and vertigo, gaze down at the rich folks in the orchestra section a mile and a quarter below, thinking, "Gee, I wish I could drop $130 a seat to be bored for 3½ hours." This might lead you to wonder why I go back at all. I go back because when it works, boy howdy, it works.

For instance, in *Les Troyons* the first act alone includes a mad prophetess of doom, the Trojan Horse, the sack of Troy, the mass suicide of the Trojan women, and, in the production I saw, Hector's young son stabbed, his body thrown onto giant hooks and dragged into the sky. Beats the hell out of *Melrose Place*. Unfortunately, the remaining four hours didn't live up to the first act. Sometimes operas peter out and don't make sense, but that's nothing new. Did anybody else see *Sphere*? At least Berlioz gave us all the blood right there on the stage. I saw the world premiere of a Finnish opera called *Kullervo* that involved the butchering of armies, rape, incest,

incest-rape, and all sorts of other juicy godawful stuff, but it all happened offstage. Every so often a character would stagger on and interrupt the chorus to sing about what a hideous mess just happened—not *here* but over *there*. I left thinking this would have been a really good opera if the stage had been built about 30 yards to the south, where all the action was taking place.

Among my favorite things about opera are the unlikely occupations assigned the characters. In *La Bohème* there's Parpignol, who is listed as "an itinerant toy vendor." Try getting unemployment from that. There's also Musetta, who is "a grisette." I thought a grisette was something you scraped off the pan after making French toast. *Hansel und Gretel* has the Dew Man, who, well, brings dew. OK, no great revelation there, but who knew there was a living in that? The sinister Skoula and Eroshka in *Prince Igor* are listed as "*gudok* players." *Gudok,* as anyone knows, is still only an Olympic demonstration sport. *The Mastersingers of Nuremberg* has Conrad Nachtigall, who is a buckle maker. My bet is he sells them in Silver Lake and the Castro. Papageno in *The Magic Flute* is a bird catcher who sings he'd rather catch a wife. I'm so sure. The man skips through the woods playing pipes and jingling bells singing "*Der Vogelfanger bin ich ja,*" the queerest aria you've ever heard.

When it comes to the music, you probably already know and like a lot of it thanks to cartoons. The only problem is that when we hear Wagner, instead of imagining Siegfried and Brünnhilde, it's Bugs and Elmer. There are other uses for opera, equally as good as cartoons. If your neighbor refuses to turn down the music that's irritating you, simply throw on an over-the-top aria (and what good aria isn't?) and crank the volume. For anyone who does not appreciate opera, Pelleas caterwauling about Melisande will more than do the trick, I don't care what music you put it up against. If you have a really sadistic streak, put on Berg's *Wozzeck*. With that score, it's no wonder the main character went crazy. There is absolutely no noise on the planet more grating than *Wozzeck,* with the possible exception of any show tune on Los Angeles radio station KGIL that involves tap dancing. (Can somebody tell me what genius decided the one thing missing from AM radio was tap?) Thank God Tommy Tune wasn't around when *Wozzeck* was first being staged.

Opera also brings out the extremes in the audience. The last time I was almost in a fistfight was at the opera. The man in front of me would not stop humming along. Did he really think we wanted to hear him and not Placido? Humming along is a pet peeve of mine anywhere. A couple of years ago I was dragged to the Hollywood Bowl for a salute to Rodgers and Hammerstein. The Bowl audience lives to hum along. You do not know hell until you are surrounded by 17,000 people humming "The Lonely Goatherd." The one good thing I can say about *Wozzeck* is that no one can possibly hum along.

There are people who have seen *The Phantom of the Opera* too many times (that would be more than once) and they sometimes sing along. The woman by me was singing the role of Christine with a voice more suited to Vera Charles. She asked if she was disturbing me. I told her yes, but I loved her work on *Maude.* Not another peep for the rest of the show.

The worst, however, is talking. Why do people pay outrageous sums of money to yammer through an opera, show, or movie? There are some acceptable exceptions, I suppose, like "Fire!" *maybe* or possibly "I'm having a coronary!" but if you feel compelled to say anything else, stay home and watch reruns of *Married...With Children* in your tawdry little trailer park. You may think I'm an intolerant elitist snob. OK, I am, but if you go with me to any performance you'll hear the show and not me exclaiming, "Look, honey, they have our dinnerware."

Actually, I've fallen out of the opera habit lately, specifically because I felt it was too elitist. The pitiful seats I could afford were so high up that I could only see half the stage. I saw *Madama Butterfly* twice but the entrance procession of relatives never because they were upstage. From where I sat for *La Bohème,* when Mimi went upstairs to her garret she disappeared among the battens. It was even worse for *Tosca,* where it looked like her lover died, she climbed the stairs up the wall, and everybody went home. What? She leapt to her death? I only heard about that on the way out—and I hate being the last to know.

GAYTIME TV

I had a terrible dream the other night. I was on *The Price Is Right*. I had made it all the way to the end by knowing to the penny the cost of dozens of common household items—a copy of Kristen Bjorn's *A World of Men* on DVD, a half-ounce bottle of Rochefort "Video Head Cleaner," the International Male gathered pouch bikini brief, a *Honcho* magazine. Now it was down to the final item. If I got it right, I'd win the grand prize: an all expense paid trip from Above and Beyond Tours to Ibiza during Leather Week and a shower with Jack Radcliffe. All I had to do was quote the correct price on Clinique Scruffing Lotion 2½ (for dry to average skin). I opened my mouth to answer, confident and sure, then hesitated. *Oh, my God. Do they mean the price at Nordstrom or at Neiman's*? I woke in a heart-stopping panic.

Although the dream had been horrible, I had to admit that I really liked like the idea of more gay-themed daytime TV shows. We could start with gayme shows. The music version of *Jeopardy!* has already been spun off to *Rock & Roll Jeopardy!* on VH1, so it's not a great reach to picture dapper Alex Trebek hosting *Gay Jeopardy!* for us.

Alex: The answer is... "He's gay." Bob?

Bob: Why did Tom and Nicole adopt?

Alec: Correct, Bob, choose again.

Bob: I'll take Hot Dishes for $100.

Alec: First time in the category. "A four-star meal."

Bob: What are the Baldwin brothers?

In most markets *Gay Jeopardy!* would be followed by *Gay Wheel of Fortune.* Pat Sajak is boring, so our version would be hosted by Nathan Lane. Since we want to be inclusive, we would also allow openly heterosexual contestants on our show. Poor saps.

"Uh, is there a B?"

"Rick, you better hope so, honey, 'cause you suck at this. OK, let's go down to the board where the lovely Steve Kelso will turn the letters. Are there any Bs? No? God, Rick, everyone at home, including your wife, has already solved this puzzle. You're losing to a circuit boy! Plus your shirt is all wrong. And don't get me started on those shoes. You wanna take a shot at solving this so we can go home sometime today?"

"Fuck you."

"No, thanks. Emile, would you like to try?"

"Sure, but I don't think I'm your type. Oh, you mean solve the puzzle?"

"Yes. You're slow, but you're pretty."

"Yes, I am. OK, is it 'Looking Through the Eyes of Love'?"

"Duh! Emile, you've won $5,000 and a European Riviera vacation from RSVP Cruises! Rick, here's a copy of *Ice Castles.* Go home and learn something."

"Fuck you!"

"And work on that pickup line. We're out of time, but thanks for watching *Gay Wheel of Fortune.*"

Why stop at gayme shows? Don't we deserve the Homo Shopping Channel? "Welcome to *The Everything Deco Show.* Hi, I'm Glenn LaDuce. You may know me from television's *Dr. Lawyer, Medicine Cop,* where I'm typecast as a gay frontier intern and paralegal bicycle policeman who's not allowed a love interest. It's a marginalized but recurring role, which is enough to qualify me as a celebrity host on this channel. This whole hour we're going to be selling nothing but clunky art deco knockoffs at inflated prices."

"And I'm Lesléa, resident hostess and lesbian shill—lipstick enough to be on camera but butch enough to make your mother squirm. Tell me, Glenn, why do gay men flock to art deco like Southern Baptists to cheap hair spray?"

"Well, Lesléa, I think it harkens back to a time when people had style, elegance, and wit. These days all we have is mousse, flavored lube, and Adam Sandler. But let's get started."

"Right. First off we have a genuine faux Erté-inspired shower curtain and matching towel set. List price is $210, but we're selling it for only $179.99. Just look at the colors. Isn't it stunning, Glenn?"

"Certainly stunned me. Especially when I learned they were made of a quality 20% cotton blend in Ghana. Let me add that these towels come hand-folded for that personal touch."

"Glenn, doesn't every gay man just have to have some fruity Erté thing in the house somewhere?"

"No, most states have repealed that law. Still, if you walk into a man's home and see a shower curtain inspired by Erté with matching towels, you can be sure that man knows how to relax a sphincter."

The next hour would be a show selling power tools. Being more of a dyke thing, Glenn would not fare so well.

"Oh, Lesléa, I love this big butch plug-in carpenter thing accessory. It has one of those gizmos that goes up and down and cuts stuff?"

"A reciprocating saw."

"Ooh, it reciprocates! So guys, you already know it's better than dating a straight man. This very friendly little number also comes with one of these scary looking jagged round...thingies."

"They're called circular saws."

"I knew that. Because they're circular and round and stuff. But who cares? Circular saws are so sexy!"

"Not when you're lisping like Cindy Brady."

"Watch it, bitch, or I'll get you back next hour when we're selling original cast albums."

"Sorry, hon. Glenn is right; next hour is *I Love a Show Tune*—somebody just shoot me now, why don't you. And if we get through that, the following hour is *Dolls, Dolls, Dolls.* See what happens when Barbie and Ken meet Billy and Carlos."

"I'm guessing Ken gets penis envy. Heck, I'll get penis envy! Ha ha ha! What are you looking at? I meant proportionally."

"Of course you did. We're going to take a short break, my sisters, then return to electrical hardware after a word from our sponsor, Snap-on Tools."

Want more? Me, too. If daytime television offered a gay talk show, I'd be there for it. Or at least tape it. Wouldn't you love coming home knowing you had recorded, say, *The John Waters Show,* with topics such as "I Used a Pump and My Weenie Exploded," or "Straight Men Who Sat on Unlikely Objects." And how about some specials? Half the on-air talent at E! are either gay or passing for it. You'd think they'd do a daytime special on the new "Men of Colt, Issue 73: Yet More Overdeveloped Guys With Shaved Butts." Still, you have to take what you can get, and so far E! is the most consistently gay thing going. They may act coy about it, but I'm certain that whoever programs E! has an Erté shower curtain and matching towels.

But all this is only cable and syndicated programming. I say we're ready for our own network soap operas. Don't you want to know who's doing what to whom on *Gays of Our Lives*? I know I'd be tuning in to Pine Valley for *Ball My Children.* (Relax, all models are over 18.) And what size queen wouldn't watch *The Hung and Restless*?

"Don't lie to me, I know you're seeing Jeff Stryker. He's putting it to you while I'm out of town, isn't he?"

"Well, it's not like he'd let me put it to *him,* is it?"

"That's beside the point. What about the twins we fathered with my lesbian stepsister? What do you plan to tell them?

"Same thing I always tell them. 'Daddy's putting *Aladdin* in the VCR and going in the bedroom with the nice man. Don't come knocking.' Besides, I happen to know you're getting it from Ryan Idol! How could you?"

"With poppers, patience, and a lot of lube, how do you think? Ah, the potential of television.

TAKE ME TO YOUR LITER

I worked for a theater company in Jacksonville, Fla., back when Carter was president and we were all going to switch over to the metric system. Our theater group subsisted on coupons for free Whoppers from the owner of the local Burger King, who was a sponsor, and CETA money. That stood for the Comprehensive Employment and Training Act, the gift of a Democratic Congress and a godsend to local theater companies and out-of-work actors nationwide. One night over Whoppers and a box of cheap wine, the managing directors of the company slapped together a proposal for a children's show, a musical no less, that would teach kids the metric system. The proposal was sent off as a joke, and damn if we didn't get a grant to do it. Now we had to write the bloody thing. I had written the book and lyrics for *A Christmas Carol,* so I was assigned to write and direct this boondoggle. This, then, is the story of *Take Me to Your Liter.*

Three school kids named Jeff, Vanessa, and Kate go into the woods to collect insects for class. While there, a space ship crash-lands and three aliens, Grick, Brack, and Fapple, emerge. They are from the planet Croutonia, which, of course, means they are Croutons—a joke that only got laughs when we played the more affluent neighborhoods. Grick is a princess who has fallen in love with Brack, a lowly palace guard. OK, by now you're wondering where the hell the metric system fits into all this. Well, the only way Grick's father, the king, will allow the marriage is if Brack proves himself worthy by bringing back to Croutonia, a world plagued by conflicting systems of measurement, a logical system the entire planet can use. Fapple is along because he is Brack's best friend and, more important, a baritone. This copious information is explained musically and at some length in what the cast called the Preceding Action Song Cycle.

The costumes for the two women playing the earthling girls were detested by both. Kate had overalls over a polo shirt, which, with her short hair, made her look like the Little Butch Dyke. Vanessa was in a skimpy little cheerleader outfit that was perpetually riding up her ass. Jeff escaped with dull jeans and a T-shirt. That was because our costumer, Randy, couldn't be bothered with him. Randy disliked Jeff intensely. Jeff was a hyperactive 20-year-old who was like Tigger on coffee and diet pills. Onstage that's endearing, but in real life it's *very* annoying. One time in the cramped company office Jeff was, well, being Jeff. Randy told him to knock it off already with the dancing and if he heard him singing "Upside Down" one more time he would throw the phone at him. Jeff sat and sulked over a magazine, but not three minutes later you could hear him unconsciously singing, "Round and round you're turning me, you're giving love instinctively..." Jeff had a bruise he had to cover with pancake for a week.

As for the aliens, Randy put them in whimsical yet skin-tight Lycra outfits that left nothing to the imagination. The actress playing Grick was a wispy 4 foot 8 but had eye-popping breasts usually seen only in adolescent boys' wet dreams. Well, most adolescent boys. Laws of physics were somehow suspended for her; otherwise she would have toppled right over. She wore massive heels and a beehive hairdo so she'd fit in with her fellow 6-foot-something male Croutons. Brack was anatomically gifted too. It was an asset he used when he later moved to Manhattan and became a minor gay celebrity with *Men and Film,* the highest-rated local cable program in New York except for *The Robyn Byrd Show.* In it he reviewed erotic male movies and was not above showing a little skin himself in sketches wherein gay porn met children's theater. I saw one segment in which he was ostensibly trying to demonstrate the proper use of a sling but kept falling down in classic kiddie show fashion and getting tangled in the chains. It was as disturbing as it was amusing. Fapple's equipment was nothing to sneeze at either, but add to it that he had a slight hernia. He looked like he was smuggling grapefruit. When these three came out of the spaceship, adults gasped and hands flew to mouths. Clearly Croutonia was the Planet of the Well-Endowed.

Kate, Jeff, and Vanessa try to help the aliens by teaching them our current English system. Everyone is happy until they discover how stupid and illogical this system is. Led by Grick, they lament with "The English System of Measurement Blues."

> I've got the English System of Measurement Blues
> The I Was Happy Till All of My Pleasure Went Blues.
> Two cups equal a pint, and two pints give us quarts.
> But four quarts are a gallon, which throws it all
> out of sorts.
> And so, we go bananas.
> We can't remember which number we're using,
> It's never the same, so it gets confusing
> Which way to choose,
> Which gives us the blues.

OK, you try writing a musical about the metric system. And add romance. Yes, third wheel Fapple falls in love with outsider Kate, and they sing a lovely song about whether the world is large enough for them to fit in. Given the prominence of Fapple's crotch, it was perhaps unfortunate the song was titled "How Big Is...?" They only sang it for the first six shows anyway because it stopped the action deader than Jonestown Kool-Aid. Children, it turned out, were not inter-

ested in my statement about interhumanoid love, self-accept-
ance, and tolerance. Fucking little bastards. So we cut the
number.

David, the man who wrote and recorded the music for
us, was terrifically talented, although he smoked great quan-
tities of pot. Once, I was driving him home and he cautioned
me on the dangers of marijuana. "If you smoke too much,"
he said solemnly, "it can really affect your...um, your...uh.
(Lo-o-ong pause.) Oh, yeah. Memory." David also had a
penchant for intricately shifting rhythms that made
Sondheim look like a hack. A single verse would see signatures of 7/8 time for a couple of bars followed by 11/13 for
a few more and then 5/9½ or something equally abstruse.
Interesting, perhaps, but a bitch to sing. Plus I had tons of
information to get across in the lyrics, so the frequent result
was something like patter songs by singers suffering simultaneously from petit mal and the hiccups. Sheer repetition,
however, saved the day on the song that was the centerpiece
for learning the metric system:

> Itty-bitty, teeny-weeny milli means a thousandth.
> Centi means a hundredth, like a penny to a dollar.
> Deci means a tenth, like a dime to a dollar.
> Kilo means a thousand, that's quite a lot.
> Remember these and you have got
> The metric system in the palm of your hand.
> Liters always tell you how much there is,
> Meters always tell you how long,
> Grams'll always tell you how heavy things are,
> As long as you remember this song. (Repeat

ad infinitum.)

We did workshops in the classrooms after the show and
taught hand movements that went along with the song so the
kids could learn the basics of metrics. Then Reagan was elect-

ed, CETA died, and everything went down the crapper. But that's another story.

OK, so the earthlings take the aliens to the library where a comic overview of the history of measurement ensues. From that they discover the elegant, easy-to-use metric system with its beautiful base ten structure, a system they can take back with them to solve Croutonia's immeasurable woes. Brack will have proved himself worthy, and he and Grick can get married. Cue taped music for the finale!

The problem was, the day before opening we didn't have a tape. Or a finale. During lunch David, in clouds of sweet smelling smoke, dropped off the performance tape. He apologized for not delivering it earlier in the day, but he had forgotten the address. Go figure. I had hoped for a simple one-minute melody that would basically be a "ta-da!" to the show. I got a five minute opus with contrapuntal voicing in $\pi/6^3$ time. But it was brilliant, so I hunkered down and wrote

> We have to leave now and go back to our planet.
> Though it's been fun here, we really have to go.
> It's time to say good-bye and not hello.

Give me a break; I was writing it over lunch and would be presenting it to the cast in an hour. Besides, I'm sure this is how Frank Wildhorn writes his musicals. The cast was happy to have anything, so I didn't hear about how lame the lyrics were for almost a week. By then it was up and running and getting good reviews, so my feeling was, screw 'em.

This show would not die. We were booked in more than 200 schools over a period of two years. By the middle of the run the cast had developed huge arms from schlepping the set around. It made the workshops run smoother, though, because it's easier to intimidate kids when you're built like the Incredible Hulk. We taught the metric system to over half a million school kids, but it was a waste of tax dollars, greasepaint, and Lycra-covered pulchritude. The country didn't go metric.

Which is really a shame. And not just because I learned it, although that should be important by anyone's account. Something like 99.99% of the countries with whom we do business use it. The metric system is simple, easy to use, and logical. Who would believe it came from the French? And still we're stuck with feet, pints, and pounds. What this country needs is something that makes people see the need for change and motivates them to want it. I'm thinking a musical.

And I see Lycra. Lots and lots of Lycra.

GAY TV, THEN AND NOW

We just got TV Land on cable, and boy, does it take me back to my tender little queer roots. Could our parents ever have known we were getting our homo jollies watching all that straight television? Whether we were getting off on Sergeant Carter or Jethro or the Hardy Boys, TV filled a void in our budding prepubescent lives that would ache until Falcon Films came along. In the meantime, though, what wonderful fantasies we got delivered right into our living rooms.

When I was little I loved *Bonanza*. Could there be a more butch paradise than the Ponderosa? Cowboys, leather, big hats, tight jeans, rugged men, leather, horses, chaps, leather, campfires, leather, roughhousing, and leather. Did I mention leather? In my dreams I was a hired hand and it was bath day at the ranch house. I got to discover the real reason Dan Blocker was called Hoss and that Little Joe had been named facetiously.

Daniel Boone had me right from the theme song: "Daniel Boone was a man, was a bi-i-ig man..." And Fess Parker in buckskin running around in the woods was all I needed to think about when Nipper Wigmore would straddle me, beating me at "Indian wrestling" in the forest behind our houses. Nipper was a bully, but as long as it ended with me being straddled, I didn't seem to mind. Isn't that sweet? My first experience as a bottom.

Another great show was *The Wild Wild West* with hunky Robert Conrad in tight little bolero jackets, fitted vests, sprayed-on pants, and, about twice a season, no shirt. I still remember one episode where James West was stripped to the waist, tied spread-eagled to an enormous gong that was going to be struck (rammed) by a giant, phallic pole when the rope holding it back burned through. Who the hell was writing this stuff, and how did it ever get by the censors? Even more memorable was the fact that James West had a big furry chest, which threw me into sidekick fantasies of being Artemus Gordon. Sure, the episodes always had some woman in allegedly alluring high-saloon getup hanging around, but in the shots of the train there was only one car for both James and Artemus, so you know that sleeping arrangements were tight. "Oh, Artie, why can't I get those women to do that!" "Because, Jim, they don't have *this*!" Cut to: Train whistle screaming. Train enters tunnel. Cue theme.

Jonny Quest was the first queer cartoon. I wanted to be Dr. Quest because Race Bannon was a dreamboat. What was going on between these two men, and why did they feel they needed their own private island to do it? "Jonny, you and Hadji go solve the mystery. I'm going into the dunes with Race!" Although I had a thing for older men, young Hadji, who was my age, also looked damn good. I think my first realization that vanilla can be boring came with the urge to tousle his turban.

Another kid my age was Eddie on *The Munsters*. I didn't want to do him, just be part of the family. If they could embrace "ugly" Marilyn, I knew they'd accept me. My parents used to point to Eddie as well as *The Addams Family* children as role models for my brother and me because unlike other TV kids, they were polite to their elders, obeyed their parents, and didn't run screaming through the house pretending to be Boy in desperate need of Tarzan. I was fine with my parents' choice of role models, mainly because the Munsters and Addamses were far more interesting than my family, although I did take a lot of playground abuse because I looked so much like Pugsley.

All this leads me to wonder what the young queers of tomorrow are fantasizing over today. On TV there's lots of future fairy fodder. It's an obvious example, but take *Hercules: The Legendary Journeys.* I love this show for the camp and sweaty Kevin Sorbo in unwashed leather, but what puts it over the top is its appeal to size queens—check out those centaurs! *Buffy the Vampire Slayer* had that cute Angel, even though being one of the undead can get in the way—and I've dated a few, so I know. Now he has his own show set here in after-dark Los Angeles and I've got yummy new fantasies of going out at night. On *Saved by the Bell* there's Ryan and Nicky and yadda yadda yadda. Give me Screech. In my experience, geeks know they have a lot to make up for and therefore work much, much harder to satisfy. I like that. Plus he wouldn't be able to be nearly so annoying with something in his mouth—say, a cookie?

For those even younger—the hatchling homos—there are cartoon characters galore to nudge that sexuality along. I enjoy watching *ReBoot* but must confess I'm in discussions with my therapist about why Bob, the Guardian, a character who's computer-generated, for criminy's sake, gives me such a chubby. (And does that make my chubby computer-generated?) There are some cartoons I find surprisingly explicit for the demographic. I mean, even I get squirmy when I see that today's Superman is practically anatomically correct. There's tight tights, and then there's being able to tell that Krypton never had a *bris.* (Then again, how *would* one circumcise the Man of Steel?) That show also bothers me because that workplace thing between Clark and Lois can't be healthy. I'm much more comfortable knowing my little nephews are watching the gay marriage that is *Ren & Stimpy.* I'd also go so far as to mention *The Tick* and say I believe Arthur and the Tick are great gay role models. One word of cartoon caution, though: Nickelodeon has a Saturday morning series called *The Angry Beavers.* I haven't seen it, but the title alone keeps me up at night. Better to stick with *Animaniacs*. Wakko and Yakko may not be all that sexy, but I think it's important to be able to laugh in bed. Finally, if I were a gay-boy-to-be watching *Pinky and the Brain*, I'm sure I'd have a thing for Pinky. No, he's not very bright, but he always gives his best effort. Plus I get the feeling he'd be open to the experience. *Narf!*

RUDOLPH THE MARGINALIZED REINDEER

I love the classic television Christmas specials that are repeated with the annual regularity of Uncle Ned passing out from eggnog. All of them, that is, except *Rudolph the Red-Nosed Reindeer*. Even as a kid I found something off-putting about it. Now that I'm grown, I recognize the problem. The dirty little secret of *Rudolph* is that it's an hour-long kiddie show about bigotry, intolerance, and thinly disguised homophobia.

Think about it. As soon as Rudolph is born his otherness is discovered, and boom, he's a second-class reindeer. His father, Donner, assures Santa, "It's only a phase," and that he'll grow out of it. Santa, who supposedly loves everyone, replies, "Let's hope so, if he wants to make my sleigh team some day." What a kick in the head to discover as a child that Santa's not a jolly old elf but a big fat bigot.

Rudolph is taught he must hide his freakishness from society when his father literally rubs his nose in the dirt to cover Rudolph's shame, vowing, "You'll be a normal buck just like everybody else." Thanks, Dad. Rudolph is outed when his nose cover falls off at takeoff practice. That's when Coach Comet announces, "From now on we won't let Rudolph join in any reindeer games." Does Donner object? Nope. Thanks again, Dad. For Rudolph the pain is so great he runs away. Ho freakin' ho.

Meanwhile, there's nelly little Herbie, who doesn't want to make toys like other elves. He wants to be a dentist. What

he already is is a twinkie to the power of ten, he just doesn't
know it yet. When the manager elf catches him playing with
dolls (hel-*lo*?) he's threatened with loss of employment.
Where is the Employment Non-Discrimination Act when you
need it? Herbie suffers abuse to the point that he too feels
there is no other choice but to run away. How many people
out there are beginning to feel like this is their story?

Rudolph and Herbie link up, as we outcasts do. They set
out for, well, I don't know, Key West. It's not only gay-friend-
ly but a helluva lot warmer. On the way they meet burly bear
daddy Yukon Cornelius. Just then the terrifying Abominable
Snow Monster arrives and chases them. Reeking of low self-
esteem, Rudolph blames his nose for the attack although,
interestingly, no one else does. The trio cast themselves adrift
on an iceberg to escape.

At this point I have to ask if the Abominable Snow
Monster was really innately bad or just troubled. After all,
don't you think that if you were called a monster or an abom-
ination it might cause issues? Oh, wait. We were. It did.
Going on.

Rudolph, Herbie, and Cornelius wind up on the Island of
Unwanted Toys. The toys are unwanted because they are different. Are you getting this? There's the train with square
wheels and the spotted elephant and a cowboy who's ashamed
because he rides an ostrich. I just want to hug him and tell him
it's OK, I know cowboys who ride truckers. There's a dolly
who looks just fine to me, she's the kind that can even say
"How do you do?" but since she's stuck here my guess is she's
a lesbian. My favorite, though, is the Charlie-in-the-Box. He
could have passed as a Jack-in-the-Box, but that would have
meant denying his true nature as a Charlie. When I was little I
thought these toys were wonderful not in spite of but because
of their otherness. They were special, not wrong. I didn't want
to leave the Island of Marginalized Toys. It felt like home. Sure,
they needed an attitude adjustment, but with some therapy this

place could have blossomed into the Castro with great skiing.

King Moon Raiser, the winged lion who presides over the island, begs our heroes to tell Santa about this place. My reaction was "Why? Santa's pretty much proven himself a couple of Christmas trees to the right of Trent Lott. Bringing him to the island would be like showing up at a circuit party with Jesse Helms."

That night, Rudolph, Herbie, and Cornelius—all in the same bed (again, hel-*lo*?)—plan to leave together in the morning. Rudolph doesn't want his nose attracting the Abominable and endangering his friends again, though, so he sneaks out on his own. It's hardly surprising. With Rudolph's overwhelming self-loathing a relationship (especially one as complex as a three-way) is going to be impossible. I'm just glad he didn't get into crystal meth, barebacking, and the rave scene. Nothing is uglier than a reindeer in a K-hole.

Rudolph goes home to face his roots, but the family cave is empty. Santa tells him, "They've been gone for months looking for you." Apparently, this year Santa is giving guilt. Santa is worried, not about Rudolph's family, mind you, but that Christmas Eve is two days away and without Donner he'll never be able to get his sleigh off the ground. It's all about you, isn't it, Santa?

Rudolph finds his family in the cave of the Abominably Abused as a Child Snow Monster, where they are being tortured and roared at. Again, no surprise. Classically, abuse victims grow up to become abusers. Rudolph charges the Abominable, only to get whacked unconscious with a stalactite. Herbie and Yukon Cornelius turn up and save the day because, with all our problems, Community does take care of its own. Herbie pulls all the Abominable Snow Monster's teeth, rendering him another societal dependent because the only thing he's good for now is putting the star on the top of the tree, and there's hardly a living in that, now is there? But I'm getting ahead of myself.

When our heroes come back to the North Pole, everybody seems surprised to see them. When it's revealed that Herbie has metaphorically castrated the Abominable by yanking his teeth out, even the manager elf is impressed. Funny how nothing gains you respect like a display of castration prowess. Two words: ACT UP.

Even Santa realizes that he may have been a little harsh, not that he apologizes or anything. At least Donner has the furry reindeer balls to tell his son he's sorry.

So everyone's kind of halfheartedly glad they're back, yeah, whatever, when Santa announces the blizzard is so bad he has no choice but to cancel Christmas. Now isn't it just like some self-important straight white male to assume he alone can put a stop to everyone's fun? Mercifully, up pops Rudolph with his glowing nose. Santa suddenly, literally, sees the light. He asks Rudolph, with your nose so bright, won't you blah blah blah. Me, I'd have told Santa to kiss my pellet popping patootie, but Rudolph has a big heart and agrees. Just before you lose all respect for him, though, he cuts a deal with Santa to stop by the Island of Underappreciated Toys and give them all homes.

So it ends with Rudolph and Herbie heroes, but you'll notice it's only *after* taking care of the Abominable Snow Monster and *after* leading the sleigh and *after* saving Santa's substantial ass. It's grudging acceptance at best, and there remains a lot of work to be done.

I hope when they get back they lead some diversity workshops and teach Santa and the rest of that cracker Christmas Town to open up and not be such bigots. Who knows? Maybe next year we'll see that Prancer and Vixen have come out as flying lesbians (their antlers being strap-ons) and that Santa has hired some Jewish, Latino, Asian, and African-Arctic elves. Now *that* would go down in history.

A ROSE PARADE BY ANY OTHER NAME

"Welcome back to the 498th running of the California Bowl of Roses Parade. If you're just joining us, I'm Bob Bluebanks."

"And I'm Stephanie Deadwards, and we're both just thrilled to bring you this creaky old parade. This year's theme is Roses Out the Wazoo. We've already seen some amazing floats and heard over 52 marching bands utterly indistinguishable from one another."

"And there's lots more to come. First though, we just received word that the Tropicana entry, 'Rosey Fruits Forever,' composed of over 8,000 crates of oranges, kumquats, kiwi, grapefruit, red and yellow peppers, and Swiss chard, collided with the Future Farmers of America float, 'We Grow Vegetables and, Oh, Yeah, Roses,'" made of two tons of artichokes, arugula, butter lettuce, dandelions, Japanese eggplant, and finocchio. Twenty-three beauty queens have been horribly crushed."

"But the good news is there's one helluva salad at Colorado and Fair Oaks. It's created quite a backup, so if you're coming to the parade, take an alternate route or bring some dressing."

"Good advice, Steph. In the meantime, here comes the Our Lady of Grotesque Suffering Marching Seminarians. These young men are in training to be priests and closet alcoholics and come all the way from Ballbound, Maine. I understand they spent last night, their first time off seminary grounds in five years, in beautiful West Hollywood."

"You know, Bob, it says here that they're over 150 strong but I only see about a dozen or so out there. What do you suppose happened to 'em?"

"I couldn't say, Stephanie. Ask your son."

"Which one? You mean Tim?"

"No, the married one. Speaking of queens, here comes the Queen's Trophy Award winner for the float that best demonstrates this year's theme. It's a magnificent rendering made of over 200 kinds of roses including Pink Parfait, Mr. Lincoln, Perfect Moment, Christian Dior, Tiffany, Irish Gold, Queen Elizabeth, and classic American Beauties, all spraying out of a great big butt. Kudos to the American Proctologists Association for their trophy-winning float."

"It says here, Bob, that the American Proctologists also chose this year's parade theme."

"There's a surprise."

"Coming up now are the Miniature Equestrian Riding Division Extraordinaire, or MERDE. They're all the way from Idaho and rode here on those adorable 18-inch-tall fully-grown horses."

"That's right, Stephanie. They keep them that small using bonsai techniques, including pruning with tweezers and nail clippers and using a number 10 rasp file."

"Aren't they just precious! You know, we should do this with children."

"I agree. The amazing float passing before us right now is entitled 'Roses of the Night.' It's sponsored by all the people who have ever played the Phantom in *The Phantom of the Opera* from New York to Bangkok. That's over 575 Phantoms, and they're all riding this float."

"And aren't they scary! My Uncle Lester used to come into my room at night."

"Did he look like the Phantom, Stephanie?"

"No, but I've been dying for a chance to get it off my chest."

"And thank you for choosing this moment. OK, this float is blaring the one memorable tune from *Phantom* and depicts the famous chandelier scene and is made entirely of five kinds of wild rice, three different sorts of dried peas, dried lentils, kohlrabi, purple kale, onion skin, and 24 varieties of dried beans. I understand that after the parade this float is going to be boiled and served to the homeless."

"Show people are just the best!"

"And following right behind them is the Marshal's Grand Prize winner for the float best demonstrating this parade's founding principle of squandering obscene amounts of money on dead plants and chicken wire."

"Bob, did you know it took more than eight weeks and 2,100 people with no lives whatsoever to put together this astonishing float? There's over $2.5 million of rare orchids, antheriums, blue iris, old-growth redwood, monkey pods, yak bane, figworts, stinkweed, and dingleberries, and the whole thing is one great honking Technicolor train wreck."

"It sure is, Stephanie. It looks like FTD threw up. While we're trying to figure out what it's supposed to be, I'm going to recite some more useless and boring figures. According to parade officials, for what this one float cost we could have paid every Israeli and Palestinian in the Middle East $100 a year not to fight, relocated Bangladesh 75 miles inland to avoid typhoon devastation, or fed 10,000 third world families and saved them from starvation."

"Oh, but it's so pretty, I'd rather have the float!"

"I'm with you, Stephanie, because if it wasn't for this spectacular parade and the terrific folks at Bowl of Roses Management, we wouldn't have this tired, overpaid gig."

"That's right, Bob. If you didn't have this, you'd be telling your grandson for the fifth time today about your pathetic glory days of sniggering game show matchmaking."

"And you'd be a local celebrity joke shilling for a dying

grocery chain. Oh, wait, even with this parade job you're still that. Never mind."

"Up yours, Bob. At least I'm still on TV."

"At least my hair is a color found in nature."

"What, shoe polish exists in the wild?"

"Bite me, you scum-sucking, bony hag with your pin-head on backward."

"Hey, wait a minute! *That's* what that float is!"

"What? Well, I'll be damned, Steph, you're right. It's a hag, she's bony, there's the pinhead, and it's on backward. And look, there's roses coming out of her ass."

"I tell you, Bob, the artistry and ingenuity that have gone into illustrating this year's parade theme knows no bounds."

"Or shame."

"But then neither do we. I tell you, Bob, I just love these floats."

"That's a good thing, because we have over 150 more to sit through and gush over. Every one more garish and a bigger overblown hoot than the last."

"So don't go away! We'll be right back with even more numbingly irrelevant coverage of the 498th annual Bowl of Roses Parade!"

PART NINE
Story Time II

LEATHERBOY ON A BUDGET

I find myself slowly slipping down the deliciously dark path that leads to leather. At times, though, I wish I were getting into something a little less expensive. Why couldn't I be getting into just being a bear cub? What I need for that I have, and it's free. Heck, I'm giving it away. It clogs the lint trap and rolls out from under the bed when people visit. But no-o-o, I have to make space in the closet for hypermasculine, hyperpricey cowhide.

Until I get my TV deal I have to buy my leather gear where I can afford it. One would think an enlightened T.J. Maxx or Marshalls would step to the fore, but so far they're only good for clothes I intend to send to my family. (I've learned if it's in a Ross Dress For Less in L.A. today, it'll be fashionable in North Carolina about the middle of next year.) So here's my leatherboy-on-a-budget confession: I got my wide black belt with the butch silver buckle on sale at Millers Outpost and my macho leather vest at a secondhand shop on Santa Monica Boulevard.

As for shoes, the last time I went to a leather event I borrowed Fred's because they had that work-boot look as long as I kept my jeans over the flashy tops. Unfortunately, they have an annoying metal piece cunningly worked into the laces that makes normal getting around impossible. I spent my night at "Manarama" walking like a Teletubby. This time I was going to wear my Reebok cross-trainers because (a) they are comfortable, (b) they're black and the bars are so dark, no one can tell if you have feet, let alone what's on them, and (c) my Reeboks don't make me walk like Tinky Winky pitching a tent. Some time ago a friend gave me a leather cap, so I was ready to go out and be butch for under 50 bucks. Little did I know there are some things on which it's best not to scrimp.

Fred's not into the leather thing, so I called my friend Martin, who is also eager to explore, and set a date for Friday night. Friday morning I spilled Fred's Catalyst Moisturizing Aftershave lotion on my one pair of appropriate jeans. (Damn you, Halston, and your cunning test-tube packaging.) I had to shower again and still only got most of the smell off me. It had combined with the soap to produce an oddly familiar scent I couldn't quite identify. At lunch I ran to the mall and bought a snug pair of the blackest black jeans—on sale for $16, what a steal. I was so pleased I only sneered for a moment when the salesman sniffed me and asked if I was wearing Jade East cologne. The pants made me look and feel so sexy I wore them back to work, without underwear. Oh, the sweet secret freedom.

At home that evening I put on the rest of my ensemble for Fred. To the black jeans I added a black T-shirt, black shoes, black leather belt, black leather vest, and black leather cap. I thought I looked *muy* macho. Fred said I looked like the Angry Gay Mime. I sulked around the house watching TV and petting the cats until it was late enough in the evening to meet Martin. Getting up I noticed my pants. Our cats' main occupations are being adorable, filling the cat box, and shedding, and given the fur on my lap you'd think I'd spent the evening shaving them. Kind, patient Fred got the duct tape, and a mere roll and a half later, I was fur-free, though residually sticky from the tape.

Naturally, I arrived at Martin's late. Just as naturally, he still wasn't ready. He warned me he'd just had the sofa shampooed, so I stretched out on the floor and cooled my heels by flipping through the latest Tzabaco catalog, lusting after the rugged, he-man model with the goatee as well as an absolutely darling origami cone light set. Martin's makeup finally jelled, and we were off to the leather bar. About the third time he yanked my rearview mirror around to check himself and preen, I had to tell him I didn't think real leathermen were nearly as concerned with Erase and plucking. He shot back that he didn't think real leathermen wore Jade East. I called a truce.

The bar was bustling, and I couldn't wait to be seen in my new stuff. I sauntered confidently over to the corner with the black light where the baddest looking men were hanging out. One of them asked if I was wearing Jade East. What the hell, I told him yeah and anybody who didn't like it could blow me. No takers, but it was still early.

Even with the odor I was getting stares and lots of smiles. Martin came by and I gloated, "Check it out, no make-up and every one of these guys is smiling at me." He whispered, "You might want to move away from the black light." He pointed down and I looked at my pants. They were covered in blazing electric white schmutz from Martin's filthy carpet. Plus, the residue from the duct tape had made me a magnet for every piece of free-floating fiber, hair, fur, cocktail napkin, and small mammal between my house and the bar. I bolted for the bathroom to brush off as much as I could, and spent the rest of the evening in the patio area.

There was to be a "Best Butt Contest" after hours, complete with a category for "Furriest," which Martin thought I should go for. I'd had three beers, and that was enough for me to agree to it. OK, so I'm a cheap drunk.

Contestants were called up to a platform, and at a signal we were to turn around and moon the judges. We had been told to have our pants undone in preparation. As I unbuttoned my no-underwear-since-lunch jeans, I was horrified to discover that the cheap-ass dye had come off on my cheap ass. I looked like I'd crawled out of a coal bin, front and back. Now, there is nothing wrong per se with a black butt. In fact, along with every other kind of *tuchus* out there, I recommend them. But a black ass on a pasty white boy is not something to be displayed. In a panic I tried to claw my way over the other contestants and off the stage, but the signal was given and everyone dropped trou except me. Living in California, there is a real possibility the ground can open up and swallow you. I was praying this would happen until I saw Martin leading the bar in shouts of "Drop 'em! Drop 'em!" Then I got angry. *All right, you asshole,* I thought, *take this.*

"I don't know why you're being so pissy to me," Martin whined on the way home as he fiddled with my gift certificate for a free piercing. "Given the dim lighting, it worked in your favor." I glared and drove on in sullen silence. "So," he said as I dropped him off, "what are you going to get pierced?"

I still haven't decided for sure, but since I've already poked holes in my nipples, I think it's going to be my wallet as a reminder to not be so tight with it. There are some things for which one needs to pay full price.

WHY WE DON'T VISIT THE REST
OF THE FAMILY

*The following Xeroxed letter was enclosed with a
Christmas card my parents received from "the old home-
stead" a couple of years ago:*

Dear Everyone,
Can it be Christmastime again? My, but it's been just a
super year, and we've been busy as bees (ha ha!). That's funny
to us because back in June we had a whole swarm take up residence in the rafters. Grandma went up to the attic after her
Hercules show to use her facial massager as usual, and the
bees attacked! She came down looking like a raspberry. Oh,
didn't we all have a good laugh!

At her funeral, grampa was a little dazed, but that was
just 'cause we'd shuttled him over from the home and he
wasn't used to all the people and sunlight. He behaved very
well, though, not once doing that thing with the Vaseline and
the hand puppet. We're thinking of letting him out again for
Christmas. Roger says if we tell him it's his birthday too, we
can kill two birds with one stone.

Aunt Esther and her special friend Ruth celebrated 20
years of friendship with a party at their house on the lake. I
had no idea there were so many artistic people up there! We
returned home just loaded down with all sorts of handmade
jewelry, macramé, and pottery. Thank goodness the weather
was nice because after all that macrobiotic food we had to

drive home with the windows down. While we were there our 18-year-old, Judy, made new friends who helped her get over her breakup with the Childers' boy, so she stayed up there an extra week which turned into three months. From all reports she was happy and so very popular! Now that she's back she seems to have given up on dating altogether for the time being. I'm sure she'll grow out of that, though, especially with the help of all her newfound girlfriends in softball. She's at a team sleepover even as I write.

Our 16-year-old, Teddy, has been very active in Future Farmers of America. Poor thing, he spent a coupla weeks in the hospital, though, when he had that unfortunate accident after hours with the automatic milking machine. I still wonder how a thing like that could happen. Oh, well, he can always adopt.

Little Edwin brought home first prize from his Bible Study. He didn't win it, he just brought it home. Still, we're glad to see some initiative after that cyber pen pal of his took him cross-country. You may have heard about it, the trial was on *Court TV*. Afterward, though, Edwin just sat in his room in the dark. I kept telling him he should go out and play and stop moping. I mean, after all, they found Edwin in the trunk of the guy's Nova, not in the crawl space with the others. Anyway it's nice to see him finally coming out of his funk and spending so much of his free time with Father Pat at church, especially since we were worried something like this might turn him queer or something. I mentioned it to Father Pat and he just smiled with a kind of faraway look, so I'm sure Edwin'll start dating soon. But just try to get him near the back of a car!

Cousin Ernie, who is so talented at curtains and wall fabrics (he won the Blue Ribbon at the county fair for his map of the United States in gingham) was abducted by aliens three times. He claims he was anally probed but didn't appear too upset about it. He says it's the closest thing he's had to a relationship since the parents of those nice Mormon boys dragged them back to Utah. Gracious, what a scene that was!

We had a big welcome-home party for Roger's sister Ida. She finished serving her sentence in May. The psychological counseling will continue for some time, which I don't understand because if you ask me, those seven people had it coming. Roger's such a worrywart, though, that when she comes over he makes the kids hide all the knives.

Also in May, Roger and I got called in for a parent teacher conference over little Petey, our fifth grader. Wouldn't you know, in one of his homework assignments he'd listed his hobbies as arson and mutilating livestock. Talk about embarrassing. I was just grateful he didn't mention the devil worship. That Petey is just a handful! I tell you, it's only a matter of time before Sheriff Harper figures out who's behind all those goats disappearing. But the Satanism seems to have given Petey some focus and it did get him off crack, so I don't want to seem ungrateful.

Oh! After all these years we finally heard from my brother Eugene! Only he's changed his name to Unit 9. He's been living with friends in a kind of retreat run by a man called Zog who really seems to have straightened him out. No more of that long-haired living in a one-room shack in Idaho sending out those scary packages. It was nice to see him looking so calm and happy on the videotape he sent (we let Petey open the package), and he looks surprisingly good with his head shaved. He said he had travel plans and promised to contact us when he got to the other side, so we're expecting a phone call any day.

Our cat Bitsy was a little firecracker this year. Four litters of kittens! Roger says he's tired of drowning them, so it was either snip-snip on Bitsy or he was taking her to the pet food plant outside of town. It was a hard decision, but we needed the money for something much more important, so we're going to miss Bitsy. We'll think of her, though, every time we look at our beautiful Princess Diana commemorative plate. Wasn't it a shame about Di? What a wonderful woman she was, even if she was dating a dirty foreigner.

Well, as you can tell, it's been quite a year for us. We look forward to the next with all its challenges, surprises, and joys. We sincerely hope you are generously blessed with happiness, love, and genetic purity throughout the new year.

See you in heaven,
The Roger Perrys (Rog, Me, Teddy, Judy, Edwin, Petey, Ernie, Esther, Ruth, Ida, and Unit 9)

ASHES TO ASHES

Neely had come to ask my friends Jim and Harvey for advice on dying. He had colon cancer, which had metastasized. Doctors could do no more than shake their heads. Neely was a musician, and as an artist, his response to dying was to make it a work of art. He was spending some of his last weeks gathering ideas from friends on how he might shuffle off this mortal coil. That is why he and his wife, Mary, had come from Atlanta down to Jacksonville, Fla., to see Jim and Harvey.

"I thought about ramming a stick of dynamite up my butt and lighting a fart," he said in his north Georgia drawl, "but with colon cancer, blowing your ass off is kinda redundant. How do you guys feel about cremation?"

"I'm for it," Jim said. "But shouldn't we wait till you die?" Harvey hit him. Neely laughed. Mary summoned a smile.

Harvey took over. "We had Lance and Edel cremated," he said, taking Jim's hand. "We couldn't bear to bury them in the yard. What if we moved?" Lance and Edel (short for Edelweiss) were Labrador retrievers from the same litter. Jim and Harvey had overfed them to the point they could hardly walk. Whenever I visited they lolled on the floor the entire time like beached manatees. Two years ago, while Jim and Harvey were on vacation, Lance fell in the Jacuzzi and drowned. As Jim put it, "Instead of returning to our children, we came home to soup." Edel refused to eat, and within a month she died too.

"Besides," Harvey continued, "as long as we don't talk about them we can imagine they're just sleeping in the garage."

"Yeah, on the top shelf under the Christmas ornaments," Jim said. "They're in little boxes, and we're in big denial."

"Neely's mother," Mary said with an edge on the word, "will want a traditional burial."

"Ha," scoffed Neely, "traditional in cannibal societies means you eat the dead guy. Let her deal with that."

"Consuming the guest of honor will make it hard to find a caterer," said Jim. "It's gonna be rough enough on Mary and Little Neil as it is."

"Where is Little Neil?"

"With my mother up in Toccoa," Neely said. "We need to get him back soon, or I won't have time to repair the damage. Last time she told him hurricanes were God getting back at Yankee Jews for coming down and buying up all the beach." He stood and hitched up his pants. "Well, we got arrangements to make and more folks to see, so we need to get a move on." Everyone hugged. Everyone cried. This was good-bye.

Soon after Neely got back to Atlanta he became very ill. He was alert, though, and planned every aspect of his send-off. He had decided to be cremated so no one would see how he looked at the end. His ashes were to be scattered off a bridge over Tallulah Gorge in northern Georgia, a beautiful, quietly spiritual place special to Mary and him. He told everyone these plans in detail and gave Mary a how-to manuscript as thick as a thesis with explicit step-by-step instructions. He titled it "Death for Dummies."

Jim was in Atlanta for a week on business when Neely died. As Neely wished, he was cremated the next morning. Also per his instructions, there was not a funeral but a memorial concert the following evening. It was a wonderful celebration of his music and his life, and it went off without a hitch. I suppose that's what comes from leaving a script. Mary, however, was a wreck, not just because of the death of her husband but because his mother, Cora, had swooped in from Toccoa. Cora was six feet of scrawny ambient anger. She had long ago subjugated her husband, Jinx, into nervous attacks, and had left him behind in north Georgia this morning to come to Atlanta and light into Mary with a literal holy fury.

"You cremated my son! You've destroyed his body, and now the Lord cannot raise him from the dead on the Day of Judgment!"

Mary explained it had been Neely's wish. She even pointed to where Neely had written—in his own hand—how he wanted his ashes to be scattered over Tallulah Gorge.

"Over my dead body," Cora intoned with a deadly look. "We have a family plot in Toccoa, and he will be buried next to his uncle Olin and cousin Pooter in the space we laid out for him when he was born. When he was alive he never did one thing I approved of," she said to her son's wife, "and now that he's dead I can finally put him where he belongs." All sanity, logic, and tearful pleading were in vain. "If you do not give me those ashes so he can be buried with his real family," she said with a steely glare, "so help me God, your son will never know his grandparents."

Horrified, Mary later poured this out to Jim, who provided her with copious amounts of tissues and vodka gimlets. What could she do? If she honored her husband's wishes, Little Neil would be cut off from his only living grandparents. As horrible as Cora was, Mary couldn't bring herself to deny her son his family. If she acquiesced, her son would have grandparents but she would be betraying her husband's explicit last wishes. Jim listened to her dilemma. Then he gave her another gimlet, kissed her good night, and went upstairs to his hotel room. Once there he called Jacksonville.

"Hello?"

"Harvey, it's me. I need you to do something."

"What is it, honey?"

"I want you to go into the garage, get Lance and Edel, and FedEx them to me."

The next day it was but little effort to dump Neely's remains into a jumbo-size Ziploc bag and Lance and Edel into the urn supplied by the funeral parlor. That afternoon Mary handed the urn over to Cora, who clutched the cremated canines with smugly victorious gall.

And that is how, a month later, Mary and Little Neil gathered with their friends on a crisp morning on a footbridge over verdant Tallulah Gorge in a beautiful ceremony culminating in Neely's ashes floating down through the light mountain mist to be received into the shimmering silver water below. And two fat dogs got buried by one skinny bitch in a family plot near Toccoa.

TAKE A MEMO

When I worked for a national glass manufacturing corporation I was secretary to the Vice President of Employee Relations. It was stultifying work, alleviated only by the occasional plant having an accident as shiveringly gruesome as only industrial work with molten glass can provide. Far removed from the plants in our Century City corporate headquarters, we were sleepwalking through our days and management could see it. They were not worried though, for in their MBA-documented wisdom, they knew how to end this malaise and improve morale. Management's miracle cure? Memos.

Suddenly, with every new hire or promotion, from mail clerk to VP, there appeared a Xeroxed stack of memos about it at the front desk. It was a grim ecological joke how many memos were written, copied, posted, circulated, and kept stocked at the receptionist's desk. Forests fell as we read about people we neither knew nor cared about. Then one April 1 there appeared the following:

To: Staff
From: Management

Management is pleased to welcome Joe Bleaux to the company. Joe brings with him many years of experience in micromanagement and advanced scratching. A graduate of Bumfuque University, Joe holds a master's degree in nostril archaeology and minored in lower intestinal biology, including honors work in inert gases. Joe most recently worked at Phleghm Co., where he held a long-standing position near the watercooler by the copy room. Joe will be spending most of his time in the ninth-floor men's room, so be sure to stop by and shake his, um, hand.

Also promoted is Shirly Chitheel to the position of director of egg sucking. Shirly is on the seventh floor, where she was formerly in charge of creating accounting errors, and she comes by her new position with minimal rug burns. Stop by to congratulate Shirly in her new job and see how it's done, folks.

Shirly replaces Dick Weed. Dick has left the company to pursue sheep. We wish them the best of luck.

Corporations have no sense of humor about this kind of thing. They lack a proper appreciation of satire. It was not surprising, then, that great wrath rattled the company from the CEO's office down. How dare some upstart alleged wag make light of management's well-considered policy of enhancing the quality of workplace life through self-congratulatory memos? All investigations proved fruitless and were doubly maddening for it. We were told we would be watched.

Rumors began circulating that the company was in for an imminent takeover. Those rumors were fanned by a memo announcing the dissolution of the yearly Bonus Committee. Rank and file resentment roiled over this. Management soon realized there were not enough memos in the world to make up for the demise of the Bonus Committee, so they came up with something better: the Fun Committee.

The Fun Committee was composed of a group of do-gooders who typically instigated unwelcome activities like Secret Santa and baby showers for detested employees. After several months of hearing about the Fun Committee's planning meetings and strategy sessions, we finally got the memo that told of the fun in store for us. It was bowling. For an office of over 200 people, it was our very own four lanes of bowling reserved for 10 o'clock on a Monday night. Tuesday morning I heard that, oddly, they only had enough people for two lanes. A month later the Fun Committee followed up with a memo, put in with our paychecks, breathlessly announcing a secret gift to employees. We had to sign up and then report to the fifth-floor break room the following Friday at 4:50 to receive this clandestine treasure. It turned out to be a card good for one (1) complimentary medium-sized beverage at the distant Westwood Burger King, with purchase. I concentrated on the irony of being able to redeem my card and, half an hour later, literally piss away my bonus. I don't believe I was the only one to feel a tad bitter about this. The following memo appeared in all the break rooms and at the front desk Monday morning:

To: Staff
From: Fun Committee

Are you ready for high jinks? Next Thursday the Fun Committee will distribute sticks of gum to all full-time personnel!

You must sign up for your one (1) stick of gum, so be sure to see Winky Fecal, who has the sign-up sheet posted on his door. The complete tally of all who will be participating in this month's Gum Giveaway Event must be finalized by close of business Wednesday so the Fun Committee can coordinate gum delivery after hours of strategizing and wanking.

Your stick of gum will be distributed at the third-floor kitchen on Thursday from noon to 12:03 P.M. A Group Chew will follow, so be sure to "stick" around! We will be announcing other exciting events in the coming months including: guided tours of the downstairs loading dock, a field trip to the drugstore for swabs, Paint Your Own Office White Day, Guess What We Did With Your Bonus, and Yahtzee!

Check one:

__ Yippee, I'm already wet! Count me in!
__ I have a written, signed, and notarized doctor's excuse.

Sincerely,
Your Fun Committee: Iggy Nimrod, Wendy Bightmee, Jimmy Jagoff, Suzie Bleauxmie, Cubbie Pockmark, Crusty Sphincter, and Tommy Rectalcoloncancer

It was not received well, neither by management nor by hurt members of the Fun Committee who could not understand why they should be targeted for spreading their corporate-sponsored tightfisted good cheer. I believe it was Suzie Bleauxmie who sniffed indignantly that some people didn't deserve next month's break room screening of *Chitty Chitty Bang Bang* at 5:30 on a Friday. I agreed with her. I certainly didn't feel I deserved it.

Takeover rumors continued, and continued to be denied. In an effort to increase cash assets—a move denied vehemently by the company even as vice presidents suddenly began exercising their stock options—lesser employees were doubled and sometimes tripled up in offices meant for one. Additionally, the supply person was so pressured to keep spending down that we were rationed such things as pens, envelopes, staples, and paper. The inevitable shortages led to desperate break-ins to the supply room just so we could get what we needed to do our jobs. An ugly and extremely official memo was issued voicing a zero-tolerance policy on pilfering to the effect that if you were caught, you would be fired on the spot. Of course, if you couldn't do your job you would also be fired—never mind that it was from lack of supplies. The following day saw this highly unofficial memo on the front desk:

To: Staff
From: Management

Because of the disappearance of certain supplies, the company will no longer purchase anything, ever again. If you cannot make do with what has been provided, the company will find someone who can and fit five of them in one office.

That is all.

This time there were angry threats of dismissal for anyone found having anything to do with these unappreciated, unfunny, and insubordinate memos. Being in personnel, I heard the CEO had ordered the computer department to go through all hard drives looking for these memos, so I warned as many people as I could. Once again time and money was wasted. Once again management was stymied and furious.

A new policy of peer review was instituted about this time. Management's version of this was to have several departments called in at the same time to a meeting in the large conference room. Because we got to start our day with this imposition, we were generously offered a meager breakfast as, one by one, the departments and the persons in them were raked over the coals in front of everyone else. Afterward it was demanded of us if we knew why morale was low. We shook our heads no, but then the following day, this memo appeared:

To: Staff
From: Management

You are cordially invited to the Conference Room for a circus of humiliation at 9 A.M. tomorrow. Please be prepared to do a public dance of degradation followed by a display of impotence and rage for the amusement of management.

A complimentary breakfast of acid coffee, heavy stale pastries, and fatty foods gone cold will be provided to make the misery perfect.

Be there or be fired.

The CEO himself stalked the halls in blustering fury over this one. Files were confiscated, accusations made, good employees threatened. Secretaries already on edge were seen running to the powder room in tears. It was all for naught, of course. To my mind it had to be someone in a position to have knowledge that such inquisitions were coming, but somehow, that was never pursued. The culprit was assumed to be a natural troublemaker, so employee records were examined. My records indicated a stellar performance. Besides, I worked directly under the VP of employee relations, a position privy to all sorts of confidential information passed between him and the CEO, so of course I could be trusted.

Then it all stopped. The CEO didn't come downstairs for an entire week. The CFO went on unscheduled vacation. Our in-house lawyer simply didn't come in. Vice presidents scurried in and out of closed-door meetings in my boss's office. At the end of the week a single memo announced that our CEO and in-house lawyer were leaving our company to take over another ailing company, presumably to make it solvent by denying supplies and bonuses to employees and flooding them with memos and screenings of *Chitty Chitty Bang Bang*.

The CFO returned with the added title of *new* CEO. Meanwhile, trade magazines made outright front-page speculations about who might buy our company. Managers were seen openly faxing their résumés. The new CEO issued a memo putting a stop to that. He firmly asserted that he was in complete command, looked forward to increasing annual profits, and that the board had assured him they had absolutely no intention of selling the company. His memo was sadly undercut, however, by the following:

To: Staff
From: Management

There have been rumors circulating about corporate shake-ups resulting from possible buyouts. This talk will cease immediately.

The flight of top company officers and the pallor of middle management is strictly coincidental. Whoever is in charge today personally assures you that there is no reason for concern. Your jobs are as safe and secure as they ever were.

Now, back on your heads.

What followed was nothing short of corporate apoplexy. The new CEO, no doubt feeling tenuous in his position and therefore more apt to be threatened by this insubordination, was livid. It was an item discussed heatedly in a meeting of the board, resulting in a decision to do away with all memos effective immediately. We were notified of this by memo.

In order to eliminate places where memos could turn up, the kitchen and break rooms were closed and cut up into offices, bulletin boards in copy rooms were removed, and a draconian set of dictums regarding what you could no longer have on your desk (no plants, no ceramic objects, no coffee mugs, no comics, one photo only, etc.) was strictly enforced. New copy machines appeared that were rumored to be able to store what was copied on them. We were not surprised when another memo appeared on noncompany paper stock. It read:

To: Staff
From: Management

The board has decided unanimously to do away with all pretense of concern for employees. Implementation of this new honesty-based policy has already improved morale—primarily among board members.

By the way, records indicate it is your turn in the barrel.

It is amazing companies don't realize that when you piss off employees they take revenge. They also take paper cutters, computer monitors, artwork, and anything else that isn't bolted down. Oh, wait, I'm forgetting the towel dispensers in the rest rooms. They were bolted down and they still disappeared. The new CEO decided he had had enough and announced one Friday that security cameras were being installed.

The next Monday, however, it was announced that he was out and a new, new CEO had been installed. To no one's surprise, except possibly the newly ex-CEO's, we had been bought. Always believe the rumors.

On Thursday the head of the company that bought our company was to visit. The new CEO put out a memo that we were to spruce up our offices and take special pains to dress and look our best that day. Follow-up announcements were made via the PA, including a suggestion that for anyone considering a haircut, now would be a good time. On top of that, the day before the visit Suzie Bleauxmie and Crusty Sphincter were deputized to go around to each employee personally saying, "We've been asked to remind you we're having a special guest tomorrow, so let's all be sure and dress a lot better than we have been lately." The next day saw a resentful staff in grudging suits, ties, and dresses. It also saw memos in 32-point print on neon-yellow paper at all copy stations, memos that were impossible for our visiting corporate *capo di tutti capo* to miss.

> To: Staff
> From: This Week's CEO
>
> The Big Cheese will be here tomorrow. In preparation, managers are to submit a list of all employees deemed to be unattractive. Said employees will be asked to remain home.
>
> Missed work is to be made up on Saturday.

Our CEO was mortified. The owner, however, merely mumbled, "Mmm. Good thinking," and continued his tour.

Over the weekend the new VPs arrived. On Monday a rumbling herd of cheery smug faces came from their new digs upstairs to introduce themselves all around in an overhearty fashion. Promises of great improvements and attention to the individual were made and, sadly, believed by the naïve. When I heard one shiny new VP, who was able to smile with his mouth but not with his eyes, actually say, "Employees are our greatest asset, right, Chief?" I knew nothing would change. I didn't care, though. It was almost Thanksgiving, my boss was already gone, and I was leaving at the end of the year.

Naturally the new batch of VPs were never seen on our floor again. Memos ceased but in their place came dry, deadly dull, ill-worded announcements over the paging system on Friday afternoons. "Christmas policy is as follows: All Jews report to their supervisors. If you will be taking Hanukkah vacation days, you will cover for Christians on December 25. The company Christmas party...what? Oh. Whatever. The company *holiday* party will be announced at this time the Friday after Thanksgiving. At that time you will inform your supervisor of your and your married spouse's plans to attend."

My quitting date narrowly averted my attendance at the company party. On my last day, this memo appeared:

To: Staff
From: Management

Nonspecific seasonal festivities will be held this Saturday evening so as to intrude on your weekend. You are requested to dress uncomfortably and parade your spouse for judgment. A dinner of watery vegetables and flesh from animals that did not die happy will be served in a rushed manner. As entertainment, the temptation of alcohol will be present. You will be jolly from 8 o'clock until 9:15, at which time you will leave or be towed.

RSVP below:

__ I will be in attendance.
__ I wish to be fired.

Merry occasion of your choice.

Some months later I heard that the Fun Committee had been disbanded by the new parent company as too costly. So much for hopes of great improvements. Suzie Bleauxmie married Tommy Rectalcoloncancer and was expecting a baby. Neither occasion, however, had been marked by an employee shower. I sent her a card and a used video of *Chitty Chitty Bang Bang*.

After I left, the underground memos stopped appearing. The person or persons involved were never caught. Don't you just wonder who it was?

PART TEN
A Final Word

RESOLUTELY FABULOUS

Some time ago I wrote a magazine piece on the art of talking to the straight person. There was something about that article that made me uncomfortable. It was a niggling thing, like the feeling I had when I returned from visiting my parents and, while unpacking, found I had only three issues of *Inches* magazine when I could have sworn I had taken four. When I saw the article in print I realized what had bothered me. I was smugly dumping on straight people like so many straight people dump on gays. So, to my straight readers, I apologize to both of you. It was wrong of me because anytime one adopts "us" and "them" language, one becomes separatist. I would never want to separate from straight people because so many provide essential goods and services we'd be lost without—among them, giving birth to queers.

Separatism was the initial issue that caused me to reread the article, but in doing so I discovered something I think is even more important. In it I commented how nothing is ever fabulous to straight people and that's what I want to talk about now. I've almost never heard a heterosexual use the word *fabulous*. How sad. Why *isn't* anything ever fabulous to straight people? Don't all God's children deserve fabulousness?

For one thing, fabulous means something far beyond the norm. If a life is lived merely normally there can be no room at the inn for fabulous. Straight is considered "normal" to the straight because there are so darn many of them, but then normalcy is nothing but numbers. According to definition, the only "normal" people are female and nonwhite and speak Chinese. That would make my dad a certifiable freak, which, believe me, would be a gift to both of us. Normal is ordinary. God save us all from being ordinary. Make me extraordinary. Just don't let me be the only one who knows it.

Fortunately for normal heteros, there are homos. It is our lot to bring glitteringly over-the-top things into being and share them with our fabulosity-challenged straight brothers and sisters. I want to say that it's the queer man's burden but that's far too sexist. And yet calling it the gay, lesbian, bisexual, and transgender burden is just too whopping big a mouthful, and we all know frustrating that can be. Suffice it to say it is a function we fulfill and a very real reason why so-called normal people need us.

So many stifling boundaries to which others feel they must kowtow are simply not there for gays. Now, there are plenty of fascinating, fun, and, yes, even fabulous straight brothers and sisters out there, but they only got that way by pushing through those boundaries. Or being pushed. If you are a heterosexual, you wouldn't be reading this if something or someone hadn't pushed your mind open a little wider. And if you are a het who has read this far, honey, I deem you fabulous here and now.

For the rest of us, though, we lucked out. Just by being queer we are automatically beyond the pale. We were born with a head start. Not to mention a penchant for lip synching. Free of "normal" barriers I can dance with the bride *and* groom at weddings, boo-hoo buckets at the movies, and go out in Lycra, leather, or latex. I have had the incredible dullness of normalcy removed for me, ironically by the normal masses who consider me abnormal. Where no rules of the normal apply, one is allowed to be anything, including fabulous. Flamboyance, darling, is born of freedom. That's why we have it. That's why those who are ordinary need it.

The class clown is always getting in trouble but is always the most interesting person in class and so desperately needed by the others. He or she is the one who pushes the envelope for everyone, creating new possibilities, new challenges to authority, and new ways of thinking. This is a role gays fulfill in society. No wonder we piss off the Religious Wrong; what could be more threatening than a new thought?

We dare to write the bitchy lines and say the unthinkable, which, in fact, everyone else is thinking but too rule-bound to risk. We dare combine a divine dusty rose with aqua *and* cobalt for a house exterior. We dare to make anorexic women go down catwalks wearing rice paper and lamp shades, then charge bored trophy wives $13,000 for the outfit. We dare to open a Broadway musical about auditioning chorus dancers with only a line on the floor for a set. *We dare.* And strangers should walk up to us and thank us for it.

At some level there is an awareness of this among the normal; otherwise why would all the fashions and fads start in gay clubs? Somebody is going there and getting what we have, watering it down so it won't scare the horses, and two years later selling it to the Mall of America by the forklift load. That two-year delay is to allow for (a) gays to move on to something even wilder so whatever's being sold no longer looks as threatening, (b) marketing, and (c) Madonna to make six videos using it.

I thank God I'm gay because it gave me a ready-made community of these outlaws who cross all ethnic and social lines. I get to meet and frolic with all kinds of colors and strata and shadings of gender, which is blessedly mind-opening too. A lot of "normal" people tend to stick to their own because they can. Little cross-pollination occurs, and that is woefully limiting. Anything limited precludes being fabulous. That goes double for closets.

Everybody at some point gets bored with themselves, even the fabulous. When you're defined as outré, whatever you do to break the boredom is simply going to be outlandish. For us, putting on Cher's "Dark Lady" and a dress is just to break the tedium. "Normal" people see it as a reason to break into television, specifically *Jerry Springer*. When normal people get bored they play hearts. Have you ever tried that? It's like root canal for four. And deliver me from Brach's Bridge Mix. But then, afterwards, when everyone's gone home, they pop in their copy of *The Adventures of Priscilla, Queen of the Desert*. Why? Because from time to time even allegedly normal people *need* a drag queen on top of a bus riding through the desert singing opera, trailing miles of silver lamé in between too many ABBA songs.

That is why it's our job, nay, our duty to be fabulous. Yes, there are days we just do not feel like spreading our wings, but lives are at stake here. So we drag ourselves out of bed, summon the muses, and create another color scheme, write another show tune, and sew another sequin. And we do it, if at all possible, someplace inappropriate or at least improbable. Don't think this isn't work, because it is. Fortunately, fabulous comes naturally to us. We're only too happy to do this for you. Plus the looks on your faces make it so worthwhile.

If you are one of the typical, the sadly ordinary, don't worry. We're here for you, always have been, always will be. That leaves us only two things to say to you poor normal people: We're so very sorry. And you're welcome.